EVANGULLIBLE

EVANGULLIBLE

WARREN B. SMITH

MOUNTAIN STREAM PRESS

Evangullible
©2023 Warren B. Smith
Mountain Stream Press
To order additional copies of this book call 866-876-3910 (U.S./CA). For international orders, call 541-391-7699 or visit www.newagetoamazing-grace.com, the author's website.

Scripture quotations are taken from the *King James Version* and are in the public domain.

This book draws upon and was inspired by some of the author's previously published writings.

The term "evangullible" was coined by Warren B. Smith in 2012. (https://herescope.blogspot.com/2012/03/overcomer-or-succumber.html).

Publisher's Cataloging-in-Publication Data

Smith, Warren B.
  EVANGULLIBLE / Warren B. Smith.
    224 pages cm
Includes bibliographical references and index.

  ISBN 978-0-9846461-7-3 (softbound : alk. paper) 1. Christianity
2. Deception 3. 1912 4. Discernment 5. New age movement

Printed in the United States of America

To Dawn

Contents

Evangelical—in, of, or according to the Gospel of Jesus Christ and the literal teachings of the Holy Bible.

Gullible—easily deceived.

Evangullible—easily deceived by teachings that contradict the Gospel of Jesus Christ and the literal teachings of the Holy Bible.

Prologue

What was once a reasonably discerning evangelical church has, in the last several decades, become a very undiscerning *evangullible* church. Choosing to be entertained rather than edified and placing a higher value on spiritual experience than on spiritual discernment, we have lost our way.

No longer contending for the faith, we are losing sight of our faith. No longer fighting the good fight, we are losing the fight. No longer warning about spiritual deception, we are becoming spiritually deceived. As a result, the true Gospel is being replaced by a "new" Gospel—a New Age/New Gospel.

Contrary to the prevailing opinion in today's church, the New Age movement never went away. Shedding its name like a snake sheds its skin, it has reinvented itself as a New Spirituality, a New Gospel, a New Narrative—a "New Christianity." However, a rose by any other name is still a rose, and the New Age by any other name is still the New Age.

Subtly, and often not so subtly, the New Age has successfully injected its core teachings, principles, and overlapping terms into an unsuspecting church. Ironically, church leaders who should have been warning about this spiritual deception are often the very ones bringing it in. As a result, the church has become filled with false Christs and false teachings.

This New Christianity/New Gospel must be exposed for what it is. If that doesn't happen, an all-too-gullible church will be walking into a cunningly devised spiritual trap—one that has been in the making for many years. And one that could come—most amazingly—in the guise of a world revival.

There shall no strange god be
in thee. (Psalm 81:9)

The False New Age Gospel

Our spiritual Adversary would have everyone believe the New Age/New Gospel that we are all "one" because God is "in" everyone and everything. Using every promotional means possible, he is attempting to convince the world and the church that while Jesus is a Christ, Christ is also in everyone. And while God is God, God is also "in" everyone and everything. To underscore this heretical New Age doctrine of God and Christ "in" everyone and everything, he would have us further believe that nothing of any real spiritual significance happened on the Cross of Calvary. However, the Bible makes it very clear that something extremely wonderful and overwhelmingly significant *did* happen on the Cross of Calvary. For it was on that Cross that Jesus Christ died to save the world as He defeated sin (1 John 2:2), death (2 Timothy 1:10), and the Devil himself (Hebrews 2:14). As the one and only true Christ, He is our Rock (1 Corinthians 10:1-4), He is our Foundation (1 Corinthians 3:11), and in every sense of the word, He is the Savior of the world.

> And we have seen and do testify that the Father sent the Son to be the Saviour of the world. (1 John 4:14)

Jesus Christ: The True Foundation

The apostle Paul proclaimed that all he really needed to know was Jesus Christ and Him crucified:

> For I determined not to know any thing among you, save
> Jesus Christ, and him crucified. (1 Corinthians 2:2)

Yet Paul also said we should not be "ignorant" of Satan's "devices" (2 Corinthians 2:11).

He further stated that it is "a shame" we have to talk about "the unfruitful works of darkness," but we must "reprove" (expose) them by bringing them into the "light":

> And have no fellowship with the unfruitful works of
> darkness, but rather reprove them. For it is a shame even
> to speak of those things which are done of them in secret.
> But all things that are reproved are made manifest by
> the light: for whatsoever doth make manifest is light.
> (Ephesians 5:11-13)

At the same time, Paul reminds us that there is a "simplicity" in Christ:

> But I fear, lest by any means, as the serpent beguiled Eve
> through his subtlety, so your minds should be corrupted
> from the simplicity that is in Christ. (2 Corinthians 11:3)

And just as there is a simplicity in Christ, there is a simplicity in the deception. Satan's deceptive scenario presents a false "God" and a false "Christ" who are allegedly "in" everyone and everything—thus providing the false foundation of a false one-world religion. Jesus warned:

> Take heed that no man deceive you. For many shall
> come in my name, saying, I am Christ; and shall de-
> ceive many. (Matthew 24:4-5)

The apostle Paul warned:

> For if he that cometh preacheth another Jesus, whom
> we have not preached, or if ye receive another spirit,
> which ye have not received, or another gospel, which
> ye have not accepted, ye might well bear with him.
> (2 Corinthians 11:4)

But what would happen if the true foundations are destroyed by a New Worldview that presents itself as a New Gospel/New Spirituality for a New Age?

> If the foundations be destroyed, what can the righteous
> do? (Psalm 11:3)

However, for biblical Christians, the true foundations can *never* be destroyed because we have "a sure foundation":

> Therefore thus saith the Lord God, Behold, I lay in Zion
> for a foundation a stone, a tried stone, a precious corner
> stone, a sure foundation: he that believeth shall not make
> haste. (Isaiah 28:16)

And that foundation is our Rock—Jesus Christ:

> For other foundation can no man lay than that is laid,
> which is Jesus Christ. (1 Corinthians 3:11)

> Moreover, brethren, I would not that ye should be ig-
> norant, how that all our fathers were under the cloud,

.and all passed through the sea; And were all baptized unto Moses in the cloud and in the sea; And did all eat the same spiritual meat; And did all drink the same spiritual drink: for they drank of that spiritual Rock that followed them: and that Rock was Christ. (1 Corinthians 10:1-4)

While many in this world build upon foundations that crumble, biblical believers in Jesus Christ have built upon a foundation that will never falter:

And why call ye me, Lord, Lord, and do not the things which I say? Whosoever cometh to me, and heareth my sayings, and doeth them, I will show you to whom he is like: He is like a man which built an house, and digged deep, and laid the foundation on a rock: and when the flood arose, the stream beat vehemently upon that house, and could not shake it: for it was founded upon a rock. (Luke 6:46-48)

However, any other foundation brings spiritual ruin:

But he that heareth, and doeth not, is like a man that without a foundation built an house upon the earth; against which the stream did beat vehemently, and immediately it fell; and the ruin of that house was great. (Luke 6:49)

The Foundation of Oneness

"Oneness" is the foundational lie of the New Gospel/New Spirituality. New Age leader Neale Donald Walsch claims to have had literal "conversations" with "God." He says God told him that

"Oneness"—God "in" everyone and everything—is the "Foundational Truth" of a New Spirituality that can save the world. In regard to this immanent, panentheistic, and heretical worldview, Walsch writes:

> [W]e see God in everyone and everything. Including our divine selves.[1]

> Oneness is the message.[2]

> It is the Foundational Truth of the New Spirituality.[3]

The following selected quotes are just some of the many ways this false foundational principle of Oneness has gradually worked its way into the world—and into the church.

The God "in" Everything Lie Through the Years

(1935) The Two Listeners in *God Calling*—Two anonymous English women claimed to receive special messages from "The Living Christ" in the 1930s. Their messages were first released in 1935 and were later turned into a best-selling book that is still popular today. Their "Christ" delivered "new revelation" that included the false teaching that God is "in" everyone:

> Wherever the soul is, I am. Man has rarely understood this. I am actually at the centre of every man's being.[4]

> I see as no man can see the God in you.[5]

(1948) Alice Bailey in *The Reappearance of the Christ*—New Age matriarch Alice Bailey and her spirit guide Djwhal Khul describe how the path to God will be based on an "immanent" God that is "within every form of life":

> . . . a fresh orientation to divinity and to the acceptance of the fact of God Transcendent and of God Immanent within every form of life. These are the foundational truths upon which the world religion of the future will rest.[6]

(1952) Norman Vincent Peale in *The Power of Positive Thinking*—In his mega best-selling book, Peale teaches the foundational belief of the New Age/New Spirituality that God is "in" everyone. He tells his readers:

> God is in you.[7]

(1971) Pierre Teilhard de Chardin in *Christianity and Evolution*—Teilhard de Chardin is called the "Father" of the New Age movement, and yet he is frequently quoted by Christian leaders. Teilhard wrote:

> I can be saved only by becoming one with the universe.[8]

> What I am proposing to do is to narrow the gap between Pantheism and Christianity by bringing out what one might call the Christian soul of pantheism or the pantheistic aspect of Christianity.[9]

(1975) The Channeled "Jesus" of *A Course in Miracles*—Oprah Winfrey stated that the New Age teachings of *A Course in Miracles*—allegedly new revelation from Jesus Christ Himself—could "change the world." The *Course*'s "Jesus" teaches that God is "in" everyone and everything—therefore all is "one":

> The recognition of God is the recognition of yourself.[10]

> The oneness of the Creator and the creation is your
> wholeness, your sanity and your limitless power.[11]

(1978) M. Scott Peck in *The Road Less Traveled*—The late mystical, pre-emergent, best-selling author and professing "Christian" wrote:

> If you want to know the closest place to look for grace,
> it is within yourself. If you desire wisdom greater than
> your own, you can find it inside you. To put it plainly,
> our unconscious is God. God within us. We were part of
> God all the time.[12]

(1980) Marilyn Ferguson in *The Aquarian Conspiracy*—The late New Age author wrote that God is "within" everyone and everything. She described God as the universal "ground of being." What heretofore had been perceived as heresy—the "immanent" notion of God "in" everything—was presented by Ferguson as new "truth." She introduced this "truth" tongue-in-cheek as "a great heretical idea"[13] that could save mankind:

> GOD WITHIN: THE OLDEST HERESY—In the
> emergent spiritual tradition God is not the personage of
> our Sunday-school mentality. . . . God is experienced as
> flow, wholeness . . . the ground of being.[14]

(1980) Maitreya in *Messages From Maitreya the Christ*—In this channeled New Age book, false New Age Christ Maitreya states that he is *the* Christ and is already here on Earth waiting for humanity to call him forth. He teaches that "God" is "within" every person:

> My friends. God is nearer to you than you can imagine.
> God is yourself. God is within you and all around you.[15]

(1980) Benjamin Creme in *The Reappearance of the Christ and the Masters of Wisdom*—Benjamin Creme, speaking on behalf of the false New Age Christ Maitreya, wrote in his book that the New World Religion will be based on the proposition that "Christ" is "immanent"—"in man and all creation":

> But eventually a new world religion will be inaugurated which will be a fusion and synthesis of the approach of the East and the approach of the West. The Christ will bring together, not simply Christianity and Buddhism, but the concept of God transcendent—outside of His creation—and also the concept of God immanent in all creation—in man and all creation.[16]

(1983) Shirley MacLaine in *Out on a Limb*—Using her celebrity status, MacLaine was one of the first people to bring occult/New Age teachings out of the closet and into mainstream society. In her best-selling book *Out on a Limb*, she and her friend David converse about the idea that man is God:

> "The simple truth," he said, "of knowing yourself. And to know yourself is to know God."
>
> "You mean that is the Big Truth?"
>
> "That's it. The point, Shirley, is that it is simple."[17]

(1987) *The Oprah Winfrey Show*—On a September 18, 1987 program titled "The New Age Movement," Winfrey praised New Age minister Eric Butterworth's book *Discover the Power Within You.* This New Age book mentions the divinity of man over one hundred times in its pages. On this particular *Oprah* program about the New Age movement, Winfrey used Butterworth to present her own New Age belief in the divinity of man. She stated:

> One of the most important books I think I've read in my life was a book by Eric Butterworth. . . . *Discover the Power Within You*. And what Eric Butterworth said in that book is that Jesus didn't come to teach us how divine he was, but came to teach that there is divinity within us.[18]

(1991) David Spangler in *Reimagination of the World*—Pioneering New Age leader David Spangler introduced the idea of "God within" as a "universal presence" and as the "ground of all being." He wrote:

> There is nothing new about saying "I am God." . . . However, in the Judeo-Christian-Moslem world, God is usually not popularly understood as a universal presence, the ground of all being.[19]

(1991) Leonard Sweet in *Quantum Spirituality*—Church leader Leonard Sweet, like other New Age sympathizers in today's church, tries to use quantum physics to allege that God is "in" everything. He makes his quantum meaning clear when he introduces the "radical" and heretical "God within" doctrine by stating that God is embodied in the "substance of creation." He writes:

> Quantum Spirituality bonds us to all creation as well as to other members of the human family. . . . This entails a radical doctrine of embodiment of God in the very substance of creation.[20]

(1992) Betty Eadie in *Embraced by the Light*—Mormon/New Age author Betty Eadie's best-selling book was extremely popular with countless undiscerning Christian readers. In describing a part of her alleged near-death experience, she writes:

> I felt God in the plant, in me, his love pouring into us. We were all one.[21]

(1992) Sue Monk Kidd in *The Dance of the Dissident Daughter: A Woman's Journey From Christian Tradition to the Sacred Feminine*—Kidd, a former Southern Baptist Sunday School teacher and now a best-selling New Age mystic, teaches the false belief of "immanence" of "God" in everything:

> Restoring the feminine symbol of Deity means that divinity will no longer be only heavenly, other, out there, up there, beyond time and space, beyond body and death. It will also be right here, right now, in me, in the earth, in this river and this rock, in excrement and roses alike.[22]

(1992) *New Age Journal* Editors in *As Above, So Below*—In this New Age book written by the editors of the *New Age Journal,* the authors discuss "transcendence" and "immanence" in regard to Oneness and the "as above, so below" idea of God being "in" everyone:

> "As above, so below: as below, so above." This maxim implies that the transcendent God beyond the physical universe and the immanent God within ourselves are one. Heaven and Earth, spirit and matter, the invisible and the visible worlds form a unity to which we are intimately linked.[23]

(1993) Eugene Peterson in *The Message*—Eugene Peterson not only uses the occult phrase "as above, so below," but he puts these

New Age words in the mouth of our Lord and Savior Jesus Christ. Instead of "in earth as it is in heaven," Peterson has Jesus proclaiming this mystical, magical, New Age phrase right in the middle of the Lord's Prayer. Also, in his *Message* "translation" of Ephesians 4:6, after erroneously translating that God is "present in all," he introduces Oneness:

> You have one Master, one faith, one baptism, one God and Father of all, who rules over all, works through all, and is present in all. Everything you are and think and do is permeated with Oneness.[24]

(1993) Jack Canfield and Mark Victor Hansen in *Chicken Soup for the Soul*—In the very first *Chicken Soup for the Soul* book, in his personally penned story titled "The Golden Buddha," New Age author and leader Jack Canfield writes:

> [U]nderneath each of us is a "golden Buddha," a "golden Christ" or "a golden essence," which is our real self.[25]

(1994) *Catechism of the Catholic Church*—The 1994 *Catechism* is the official source for Roman Catholic doctrine. The following quotes are taken straight from the *Catechism*:

> Let us rejoice then and give thanks that we have become not only Christians, but Christ himself. Do you understand and grasp, brethren, God's grace toward us? Marvel and rejoice: we have become Christ. (#795)[26]

> For the Son of God became man so that we might become God. (#460)[27]

> The only-begotten Son of God, wanting to make us sharers in his divinity, assumed our nature, so that he, made man, might make men gods. (#460)[28]

(1996) Neale Donald Walsch in *Conversations With God: Book 1*— The New Age "God," speaking through Walsch, tells everyone:

> You are already a God. You simply don't know it.[29]

(1997) Henri Nouwen in *Here and Now*—Henri Nouwen, the late Catholic mystic, is frequently quoted by undiscerning pastors and Christian leaders. In his book, *Here and Now*, Nouwen writes:

> The God who dwells in our inner sanctuary is also the God who dwells in the inner sanctuary of every human being.[30]

(1999) Leonard Sweet in *soulTsunami*—With a front cover endorsement by Rick Warren of Sweet's book *soulTsunami*, New Age sympathizer/church leader Leonard Sweet introduces the New Age concept of "immanence" after suggesting that Christians "learn to speak out of both sides of the mouth":

> To survive in the postmodern culture, one has to learn to speak out of both sides of the mouth . . . Biblical theological is not circular with a fixed center, but elliptical, revolving around the double foci of God's immanence and God's transcendence.[31]

(2002) Rick Warren in *The Purpose-Driven Life*—In *The Purpose Driven Life*, Rick Warren quotes Ephesians 4:6 from a *New Century Bible* translation, which erroneously states that God is "in" everything:

> Because God is with you all the time, no place is any closer to God than the place where you are right now. The Bible says, "He rules everything and is everywhere and is in everything."[32]

(2003) Robert Schuller in an *Hour of Power* Sermon—On November 9, 2003, using the same overlapping New Age term of "immanence," Robert Schuller told his international television audience that God was an immanent God because he was "in every single human being":

> The immanence of God means here, in me, around me, in society, in the world, this God here, in the humanities, in the science, in the arts, sociology, in politics—the immanence of God. . . . Yes, God is alive and he is in every single human being.[33]

(2003) Tom Holliday and Kay Warren in their Saddleback Church *Foundations Participants Guide*—Invoking the same overlapping concept of "immanence," the *Foundations Participants Guide* states:

> The fact that God stands above and beyond his creation does not mean he stands outside his creation. He is both transcendent (above and beyond his creation) and immanent (within and throughout his creation).[34]

(2004) Sarah Young in *Jesus Calling*—The July 8th message on page 199 that Sarah Young says she received from "Jesus" states that He is "in" everything:

> I am above all as well as in all.[35]

(2006) Rhonda Byrne in *The Secret*—This New Age author prominently features the occult/New Age phrase "as above, so below" at the front of her book. On page 164, the term is explicitly defined:

> You are God in a physical body.[36]

(2006) *What the Bleep Do We Know!?*—This popular New Age movie featured in theaters across the country tried to use quantum physics to convince people that God is "in" everyone and everything. New Age channeler J. Z. Knight appears in the film and channels an alleged "spirit guide" named Ramtha. This spirit guide proclaims that quantum physics proves that we are all "God."

> We have the epitome of a great science . . . quantum physics . . . Everyone is God.[37]

(2006) Elizabeth Gilbert in *Eat, Pray, Love*—In this best-selling New Age book, Gilbert frequently references the idea that God is "in" everyone. For example, she writes:

> God dwells within you as yourself, exactly the way you are. . . . To know God, you need only to renounce one thing—your sense of division from God.[38]

(2007) William Paul Young in *The Shack*—Like many New Age proponents, author William Paul Young uses the term *ground of being*. In this book that was enthusiastically read by millions of un-suspecting Christians, Young's "Jesus" uses the phrase to underline his heretical statement that God is "in" all things:

> God who is the ground of all being, dwells in, around, and through all things.[39]

(2011) Glenn Beck in *The Seven Wonders That Will Change Your Life*—He writes:

> If God is everything and everywhere and inside everyone, then I figured He had to be inside me, too.[40]

(2016) Pope Francis—A November 1, 2016 *Catholic News Service* article titled "Pope Offers New Beatitudes for Saints of a New Age" quotes Pope Francis stating that God is "in" everyone:

> Blessed are those who see God in every person and strive to make others also discover him.[41]

(2018) Matthew Fox—This New Age leader and author of *The Coming of the Cosmic Christ* features the following statement on his website:

> In Creation, God is both immanent and transcendent. This is panentheism which is not theism (God out there) and not atheism (no God anywhere). We experience that the Divine is in all things & all things are in the Divine.[42]

(2018) Roma Downey—In an interview about her 2018 book *Box of Butterflies*, the Catholic New Age sympathizer actress stated the following when asked why the presence of God is important. She said:

> God is everywhere, in everyone, in everything we do.[43]

(2019) Richard Rohr—In his best-selling book *The Universal Christ,* this popular Catholic Franciscan priest writes:

> A mature Christian sees Christ in everything and everyone else.[44]

(2023) The Catholic Jesuit organization—The heading of their global website states:

> Finding God in all things.[45]

Scriptural References to Show God is *Not* "in" Man

There shall no strange god be in thee. (Psalm 81:9)

Thou shalt have none other gods before me. (Deuteronomy 5:7)

Put them in fear, O LORD: that the nations may know themselves to be but men. (Psalm 9:20)

. . . verily every man at his best state is altogether vanity. (Psalm 39:5)

I am the LORD: that is my name: and my glory will I not give to another. (Isaiah 42:8)

I am the LORD, and there is none else, there is no God beside me: I girded thee, though thou hast not known me: That they may know from the rising of the sun, and from the west, that there is none beside me. I am the LORD, and there is none else. (Isaiah 45:5-6)

Shall a man make gods unto himself, and they are no gods? (Jeremiah 16:20)

Son of man, say unto the prince of Tyrus, Thus saith the Lord GOD; Because thine heart is lifted up, and thou hast said, I am a God, I sit in the seat of God, in the midst of the seas; yet thou art a man, and not God, though thou set thine heart as the heart of God. (Ezekiel 28:2)

I will not execute the fierceness of mine anger, I will not return to destroy Ephraim: for I am God, and not man; the Holy One in the midst of thee: and I will not enter into the city. (Hosea 11:9)

And whosoever shall exalt himself shall be abased; and he that shall humble himself shall be exalted. (Matthew 23:12)

But Jesus did not commit himself unto them, because he knew all men, And needed not that any should testify of man: for he knew what was in man. (John 2:24-25)

And again, The Lord knoweth the thoughts of the wise, that they are vain. Therefore let no man glory in men. (1 Corinthians 3:20-21)

. . . that ye might learn in us not to think of men above that which is written, that no one of you be puffed up for one against another. (1 Corinthians 4:6)

For we preach not ourselves, but Christ Jesus the Lord; and ourselves your servants for Jesus' sake. (2 Corinthians 4:5)

For if a man think himself to be something, when he is nothing, he deceiveth himself. (Galatians 6:3)

Final Thoughts

It has been rightly said that God is God and we are not. However, strong pressure is being continually mounted to convince everyone there is a New Age/New Gospel/New Spirituality/New Worldview that can save the world from its present problems. We are being told that if we "awaken" to the "new revelation" that "we are all one" because "God is in everyone and everything" then world peace can happen. But we know from Scripture that a false Christ—Antichrist—"shall destroy wonderfully, and shall prosper, and practice" and "by peace shall destroy many" (Daniel 8:24-25). The Bible warns that what will one day appear to be a wonderful "peace and safety" will suddenly turn into terrible "destruction" (1 Thessalonians 5:3).

Universal Oneness is obviously a *broad* way. However, the true Christ—Jesus Christ—warns that "broad is the way, that leadeth to destruction" (Matthew 7:13). He also warns that *narrow* is the way "which leadeth unto life, and few there be that find it" (Matthew 7:14). He later states a time will come when Satan, working through Antichrist, will deceive "the whole world" (Revelation 12:9).

Describing the coming apostasy, the apostle Paul says that people "received not the love of the truth, that they might be saved" and "believed not the truth" (2 Thessalonians 2:10-12). Thus, with "itching ears," humanity will "turn away their ears from the truth" (2 Timothy 4:3-4) as they turn toward things like a New Age/New Gospel/New Spirituality that teaches we are all "one" because God is "in" everyone and everything.

God is not impressed with deceptive devices like worldly Oneness and neither should anyone who reads and believes the Bible. Genesis 11:6 records what the Lord has to say about worldly Oneness:

> Behold, the people is one, and they have all one language; and this they begin to do: and now nothing will be restrained from them, which they have imagined to do.

Scripture records that God was so displeased with their contrived Oneness that He confounded their language and scattered them all over the face of the Earth (Genesis 11:7-8). Contrast this with Galatians 3:26-28 where the apostle Paul says to those who are actual believers, "Ye are all one in Christ Jesus." He does not say that Christ is "in" everyone. Rather, He says that everyone who believes in Jesus Christ is "one" in Christ. In Ephesians 1:1 and 4:6, Paul tells believers at the church in Ephesus and the "faithful in Christ Jesus" that God is in "you all" solely by virtue of their belief. God does not naturally reside in everyone and everything. Thus, a big difference exists between the mistaken notion of universal worldly Oneness and believers who become "one" in Christ through their belief and faith in the true Jesus Christ.

Acts 17:26 affirms that all of humanity is "one blood" because we come from an original set of parents—Adam and Eve. But "That which is born of the flesh is flesh; and that which is born of the Spirit is spirit" (John 3:6). That is why Jesus said—"Ye must be born again" (John 3:7). It is only after conversion to the true Jesus Christ that the Holy Spirit is sent to believers. As a result of that commitment and conversion, it can be said that God is now "in" those believers. But those believers are not God. And most certainly, God is not "in" everyone and everything.

Years ago, people claiming to be God were considered delusional. The way things are going, it may not be long before those who know they are *not* God will be the ones who are considered delusional. It has been said that when a lie is told often enough and long enough, over time it will eventually be perceived as truth. Because most Christians are not contending for the faith, the big lie that "God is in everyone and everything" is fast becoming the new spiritual norm. Consequently, one can see how evil may soon rule the world—just as the Bible said it would. And it may be a lot sooner than most people would ever imagine.

> Who changed the truth of God into a lie, and worshipped and served the creature more than the Creator, who is blessed for ever. Amen. (Romans 1:25)

And the LORD said, Behold, the people is one, and they have all one language; and this they begin to do: and now nothing will be restrained from them, which they have imagined to do. (Genesis 11:6)

2

Oneness vs. Separation Heresy

On the March 12, 2017 episode 5 of Trinity Broadcasting Network's *Restoring The Shack* twenty week television series,[1] *The Shack* author William Paul Young stated that it is a "lie" to believe that God is "separate" from His creation.[2] Invoking a vision that was reputedly given by God to his friend and fellow author C. Baxter Kruger, Young described this alleged lie as the "lie of separation." But as a former New Ager, I recognized that what Young was calling the "lie of separation" was in and of itself a lie. What he was teaching had nothing to do with biblical Christianity and everything to do with the deceptive antichrist teachings of the New Age/New Spirituality/New Worldview.

What Young was attempting to convey to countless TBN viewers was the same thing I had been taught when I was part of the New Age movement—that "we are all one" and there is "no separation" between God and creation because God is "in" everyone and everything. But God is *not* "in" everyone and everything.[3]

As my wife and I came out of the New Age and saw through this pervasive deception, we came to understand how our spiritual Adversary had twisted the Bible's 2 Corinthians 6:17 instruction to "be ye separate" into a lie that turns the whole notion of

31

biblical separation upside down. Now, years later, taking the word "separation" and using it in a wholly unscriptural context, professing Christians like William Paul Young are now bringing this New Age "lie of separation" into the church.

The God "in" Everything Heresy

As explained in chapter one, this heretical teaching that God is "in" everything—and therefore not separate from His creation—is *the* foundational doctrine of the New Age/New Spirituality/New World Religion.[4] This heretical teaching is taught in William Paul Young's best-selling novel, *The Shack* when Young's cleverly contrived "Jesus" states:

> God, who is the ground of all being, dwells in, around, and through all things.[5]

However, most people reading *The Shack* don't understand that this statement is an unbiblical New Age lie. Yet Young puts this false teaching right in the mouth of *his* "Jesus." Thus, by virtue of this occult utterance alone, it becomes immediately evident that Young's "Jesus" is a false Jesus—"another Jesus" (2 Corinthians 11:4)—who is *not* representative of the real Jesus Christ. *Shack* readers should also note that Young never identifies his "Jesus" as Jesus *Christ*. In fact, the word "Christ" cannot be found anywhere—not even once—in Young's whole *Shack* story.

The False Doctrine of Oneness

Because God was said to be "in" everyone and everything, our New Age teachers taught us that we were all "One" and that our Oneness with God—our *union* with God—connected us to everyone and everything. We were told that because of this Oneness connectivity, there was—therefore—no separation between God and creation. And so it was this concept of Oneness that singularly expressed our New Age belief in the "universal" divinity of all things. It seemed logical. We were all One because we were all connected—in *union* with God—because we thought God was "in" everyone and everything. We were all New Age universalists because we honestly believed that a universal acceptance of this universal teaching would bring a universal peace to a hurting world.

Completely deceived by this New Age lie, we sensed that humanity was beginning to "awaken" and "shift" into accepting this "emerging" concept of "universal Oneness." We believed if this New Age/New Gospel of humanity's innate divinity was passionately, wholeheartedly, and universally embraced by all the world's religions, it could save the world.

Contrarily, those who refused to subscribe to this New Worldview of universal Oneness would significantly hinder—and ultimately prevent—the attainment of this otherwise realizable goal of what was being described by our New Age teachers as "God's Dream" for world peace. The false New Age "God" and "Christ"—channeling through their designated New Age leaders— specifically warned that the only people who stood in the way of world peace were those who were stuck in their own delusional dreams of separation—who had been deceived into believing the "lie of separation." But what New Age leaders were teaching about separation was the *real* lie.

The False Doctrine of Separation

This deceptive New Age "lie of separation" was cunningly devised by the father of lies. Its purpose is to isolate, denigrate, and ultimately persecute those who do not believe that God is "in" everyone and everything. To not believe that is to not believe that everything is "connected" and "divine" and "One." To not believe that everything is "connected" and "divine" and "One" is to not believe in Oneness. To not believe in Oneness is to believe in "the lie of separation." It is all a very seductive and devilish spiritual trap. And the false New Age "Christ" warns that the consequences for those who ultimately refuse to believe that God is "in" everyone and everything will be extremely severe.

Oneness vs. Separation Deception

Thus, from a New Age perspective, "Oneness vs. Separation" juxtaposes two prevailing but opposing worldviews against each other. Oneness, being hailed as the "loving" and *spiritually correct* worldview, will produce global unity, world peace, and a "happy" humanity. To the contrary, "separation" is described as a "hateful" and *spiritually incorrect* worldview that prevents global unity, prevents world peace, and produces a "fearful" and "unhappy" humanity. As seen in the quotes below, the false New Age "Christ" makes his strategic case for Oneness while simultaneously threatening those who subscribe to what he calls the "sin" and "hatred" of "separation." This false Christ states:

> The recognition of God is the recognition of yourself. There is no separation of God and His creation.[6]

> The oneness of the Creator and the creation is your wholeness, your sanity and your limitless power.[7]

> Let us together show the world: that the need for war is past; that the instinct of man is to live and to love; that hatred is begotten of separation.[8]

> I shall drive from this Earth forever the curse of hatred, the sin of separation.[9]

Separation Is Satan?

In the New Age, we didn't believe in an actual Devil—a real Satan. The only thing that was said to be "satanic" was to not believe in the divine Oneness of all creation. The only "Satan" were those people who had been deluded into believing the "lie of separation"—the belief that God was not "in" everyone and everything. Thus, the New Age "God" and "Christ" equate Satan with anyone who refuses to submit to their antichrist "Doctrine of Oneness." Consequently, biblical Christians become a specific and immediate target as they are conveniently and diabolically labeled as being under the "illusion" of a lie—the "lie of separation." The New Age "God" and "Christ" boldly and blasphemously state:

> The mind can make the belief of separation very real and very fearful, and this belief is the "devil."[10]

> When at last you see that there is no separation in God's World—that is, nothing which is not God—then, at last, will you let go of this invention of man which you have called Satan.[11]

> Your triumph over Satan, that is, over the illusion of separation, will be a victory for the universal community.[12]

Thankfully, I was ultimately shown that while God is near and ever-present, He is not "in" everyone and everything. And while He is definitely separate from His creation, His Holy Spirit *is* sent to dwell within those who repent of their sins and confess the true Jesus Christ. However, those who accept the true Jesus Christ are *not* divine or in any way God or God Himself. Thus, I came to realize that this heretical God "in" everything Doctrine of Oneness was the real lie. But most Christians watching TBN's *Restoring The Shack* television series had no idea that the "lie of separation" Young introduced on that program was devised by a deceptive false Christ and was totally fraught with New Age meaning.

"Dam" Vision/Damnable Heresy

As I watched that fifth episode of *Restoring The Shack* on TBN, I could see how William Paul Young used the same spiritual terminology that paralleled—and directly dovetailed—with the heretical New Age Doctrine of Separation. Young tried to make his case for the "lie of separation" by recounting what friend and fellow author C. Baxter Kruger said he was shown in a vision that was allegedly from the Lord. Young stated:

> And Baxter had a visual, and he was looking at this massive mountain range, and he could see a beaver dam that was big enough to block the entire Mississippi—massive—and he asked the Lord, "What is that?"
>
> And he heard the response inside his heart, "That is the lies of pastors and theologians and the institutional church system that has been damming up the rivers of living water in the western world."
>
> And Baxter was looking at the very bottom where these huge monster redwoods—and there was one at the center of the bottom, and Baxter said, "What is *that?*"
>
> And he heard, "That Baxter is the *lie of separation*. The western world has convinced itself that it has separated itself from God. There has never been separation. That is absolutely a myth. You take that one out, and the whole beaver dam will start to crumble." Because for a lot of us, the gospel was about separation. That was the assumption.[13]

Unbelievable! Young was telling countless Christian viewers that Kruger's vision came directly from the Lord—that it was God Himself who told Kruger it is the "lie of separation" that has undermined the true Gospel and is "damming up the rivers of living water in the western world." Yet this was exactly what we had been taught by the New Age "God" and "Christ." Same terminology. Same concept. Same deception.

Deceived and Deceiving

True to the Bible's warning, William Paul Young and C. Baxter Kruger were "deceiving, and being deceived" (2 Timothy 3:13) as they presented Kruger's *alleged* revelation from the Lord. But what Kruger saw and heard in his vision and what William Paul Young passed on to TBN viewers was *not* from our one true Lord. Absolutely no way. Having come out of the New Age movement with all its spiritual deception, I learned the hard way that voices purporting to be from God can be "seducing spirits" bringing "doctrines of devils" (1 Timothy 4:1)—like the heretical New Age/New Gospel doctrines of Oneness and Separation.

There is a Deceiver, and the Bible warns us to "believe not every spirit, but try the spirits whether they are of God: because many false prophets are gone out into the world" (1 John 4:1). The voice C. Baxter Kruger heard was teaching the same thing that the false New Age Christ taught us in the New Age about separation. Kruger's alleged vision from "the Lord"—this purported "lie of separation"—was setting the church up for the *real* lie—the heretical lie of Oneness vs. Separation. And this is exactly what the apostle Peter is describing when he warns about "cunningly devised fables" like *The Shack* (2 Peter 1:16) and "damnable heresies" (2 Peter 2:1) like the "lie of separation" that would be brought in by "false teachers among you." What irony that it is Kruger's "dam" vision that Young uses to present this "damnable" heresy regarding separation.

> But there were false prophets also among the people, even as there shall be false teachers among you, who privily shall bring in damnable heresies. (2 Peter 2:1)

Same Separation Language

It is important to note the obvious similarities between the "lie of separation" concept Young and Kruger attribute to the Lord and the New Age "lie of separation" concept. The following are several more examples of what the New Age "God" and "Christ" have stated about separation:

> A sense of separation from God is the only lack you really need correct.[14]

> The only solution is the Ultimate Truth: nothing exists in the universe that is separate from anything else.[15]

> This is your assignment. This is your work. You are to destroy the illusion of separation.[16]

Separation and Sickness

The New Age "Jesus" teaches that sickness results from believing you are "separate" from God. Healing—according to this New Age "Jesus"—comes from recognizing and rejecting the "lie of separation" and believing in the truth of Oneness instead. He states:

> A sick person perceives himself as separate from God. Would you see him as separate from you? It is your task to heal the sense of separation that has made him sick.[17]

William Paul Young's *Shack* therapy, for what he describes as his own and the world's "Great Sadness," parallels this New Age healing proposed by the channeled teachings of the New Age "God" and "Christ." Young and Kruger—like their New Age counterparts— would have the church "awaken" from the "lie of separation" and "shift" into seeing that God is at "One" and in "union" with everyone and everything. But this *Shack* therapy is a heretical antichrist therapy that is not from the one true God.

C. Baxter Kruger

For those not familiar with C. Baxter Kruger, he is a self-described Mississippi theologian who is the Director of Perichoresis Ministries and the author of nine books that include *The Shack Revisited: There Is More Going on Here Than You Ever Dared to Dream* (2012). A number of his many joint speaking appearances with William Paul Young are easily found on the Internet. In his introduction to *The Shack Revisited*, Young writes that Kruger's book will help the reader to better understand the "perspectives and theology that frame *The Shack*."[18] While Kruger's account of the beaver dam vision and the "lie of separation" don't appear in his book *The Shack Revisited*, they do show up in Kruger's 2016 book *Patmos*.

In *Patmos*, Aidan, "a burned-out, suicidal theologian" from Mississippi, time travels to the first century and lands in a cave with the apostle John. Kruger conveniently puts *his* own words and *his* own theology in John's mouth—much like Young did with "Papa," "Jesus," and "Sarayu" in *The Shack*. By the end of his novel, Kruger transforms the apostle John into an apostate John—most especially when it comes to a conversation Aidan and John have regarding separation. After Aidan tells John how he had to "escape the twin clutches of fundamentalism and modernism,"[19] Kruger's John tells him, "There is only one battle"—"Union or separation."[20] He tells Aidan that the world's problems all revolve around one crucial matter—"Ourselves and our ideas about *separation* from God."[21] Kruger's apostle John then contrasts the Oneness that comes from believing that Jesus is "in" everyone with the "lie of separation." Kruger's John gives the time traveling Aidan the following New Age/New Gospel message:

[The] lie of separation from God is the chief of all lies.[22]

Dear brother, either Jesus is in us or we are separated from him.[23]

At one point, Aidan asks John:

This mess, this historical quagmire of religions, wars, abuses, lust, and fear, all grows out of a single untruth?

John answers Aidan:

Indeed my son. . . . The lie that we are separated from Jesus and his Father.

Aidan responds:

So in your gospel and letters, you're trying to help us see through the lie of separation.[24]

In another exchange, John tells Aidan, "The assumption of separation is the great darkness."[25] Never referring to Satan as Satan, but only as "Ophis," Kruger's "John" makes it look like the "lie of separation" is at the heart of Satan's scheme to deceive the world:

This is Ophis's chief trick—blind us to how close the Lord is, closer than breath: we're in him, and he's in us. Ophis deceives the nations by one lie—separation. [26]

Talks Like New Age

Thus Kruger—by putting his own words in the apostle John's mouth—has John teaching what the New Age has been teaching for decades—that there is no separation between God and His creation because God is "in" everyone and everything. But what Kruger is teaching is not true and not from God. He and William Paul Young are *not* exposing the deception—they are part of it. The *real* lie that is in the process of deceiving the world *and* the church is Oneness. And again, this just happens to be what *The Shack*'s "Jesus" tells *Shack* readers when he authoritatively states:

> God, who is the ground of all being, dwells in, around, and through all things.[27]

The parallels between what the New Age is saying about Oneness and Separation and what Kruger and Young are saying should be deeply disturbing to anyone who loves the truth. And while Young and Kruger would probably deny that what they are teaching is New Age, it is a simple matter of semantics. Once again, a rose by any other name is still a rose, and a "God" who "dwells in, around, and through all things" is still the false New Age "God" of universal Oneness.

The Selection Process

The upshot of all this upside-down twisted teaching is that one day people may very well live or die based on what they believe regarding the battle between Oneness and Separation. The false New Age Christ threatens that there will be no place in the future for those who are into separation—those who know that God *is* "separate" from His creation because they know that God is not "in" everyone and everything. In my book *False Christ Coming: Does Anybody Care?*, I described how this false New Age Christ warns that those who refuse to subscribe to his gospel of Oneness will be handed over to his deadly "selection process." He states:

> Dearly beloved, I approached the crucifixion far more easily than I approach the selection. The crucifixion was done unto my body. The selection will be done unto yours.[28]

> Cynics, disbelievers, those who fear and cannot love:
> know that the mercy of God almighty is with you now.
> The second death, for you, is a purification, an erasing
> of the memory of fear, through the shock of a fire.[29]

> [T]he fundamental regression is self-centeredness, or
> the illusion that you are separate from God. I "make
> war" on self-centeredness.[30]

> At the co-creative stage of evolution, one self-centered
> soul is like a lethal cancer cell in a body: deadly to itself
> and to the whole.[31]

> The surgeon dare leave no cancer in the body when he
> closes up the wound after a delicate operation. We dare
> leave no self-centeredness on Earth after the selection
> process.[32]

> The crime of separation, of division, of lawlessness must
> go from the world. All that hinders the manifestation
> of man's divinity must be driven from our planet. My
> Law will take the place of separation.[33]

> I shall drive from this Earth forever the curse of ha-
> tred, the sin of separation.[34]

Thus, separation becomes a pejorative and pernicious label to denigrate and persecute anyone who refuses to subscribe to the Doctrine of Oneness. The huge sign of the times is that what was being pushed by New Age leaders in the world is now being pushed by men like William Paul Young, C. Baxter Kruger, and other professing Christians in the church.

Far from disappearing, the New Age is now charging full steam ahead into the church through books like *The Shack* and "Christian" television programs like TBN's *Restoring the Shack*. In the meantime, the Bible warns us not to be deceived by men who come in the name of Christ but who are "deceiving, and being deceived" (2 Timothy 3:13)—and who in the name of Christ are actually opposing Christ.

The First Commandment states we are to have no other gods before us. But the "God" of Oneness—this "God" who is "in" everyone and everything—is another god, a completely different god, a false God. No matter how much the church may want to deny or ignore it, there is a false Christ coming, and the way is already being prepared for his ultimate appearance. *The Shack* is much more than a "bad" book—it is the breath of Antichrist as he descends on a church that is all too gullible and fast asleep.

Blessed are ye, when men shall hate you, and when they shall separate you from their company, and shall reproach you, and cast out your name as evil, for the Son of man's sake. (Luke 6:22)

Lest Satan should get an advantage
of us: for we are not ignorant of his
devices. (2 Corinthians 2:11)

"God's Dream"–
The Ultimate Scheme

Google the term "God's Dream," and you will immediately find countless references on Christian websites to this popular spiritual term. An ever-increasing number of Christian authors, pastors, youth leaders, evangelists, bloggers, musicians, and everyday believers are using the term "God's Dream" as if it has some sound scriptural basis. It doesn't. Keep looking, and you will find that the concept of "God's Dream" is also presented by a wide variety of New Age leaders, authors, gurus, bloggers, and false Christs. Most Christians using the concept of "God's Dream" are unaware it is an overlapping New Age term that can be traced at least as far back as the early 1900s where it was referenced in two New Age magazines published for those interested in the occult teachings of Theosophy and the coming of a false Christ named Maitreya.

In reality, "God's Dream" is a devilish scheme cunningly devised by our spiritual Adversary to meld together two otherwise irreconcilable worldviews—New Age universalism and biblical Christianity. The unstated purpose in the popularization of the term "God's Dream" is to provide all religions and all peoples with a shared "we have a dream" rallying cry for the cause of Oneness and *spiritual integration* extracted and borrowed from Martin Luther King's "I have a dream" rallying cry for *racial integration*.

A New Age Civil Rights Movement

New York Times best-selling author and New Age channeler, Neale Donald Walsch, writes that "God" personally told him that the New Age/New Spirituality is a divinely inspired "civil rights movement for the soul." "God" tells Walsch:

> I have said repeatedly that the New Spirituality is a civil rights movement for the soul.[1]

However, this "civil rights movement for the soul" is, in reality, a deceptive New Age Peace Plan that seeks to undermine and ultimately destroy biblical Christianity. Walsch states that this "God's Dream" Peace Plan will become an accomplished fact when humanity self-realizes we are all "One" because God is "in" everyone and everything. Walsch writes:

> God's "dream," if you please, is that we will all one day be completely realized [as "God"].[2]

Martin Luther King Jr.

To promote this "God's Dream" "civil rights movement for the soul," New Age leaders are in the process of co-opting Martin Luther King Jr.'s inspirational "I have a dream" theme for their own "We have a dream"—"God's Dream"—New Age purposes. Twisting King's impassioned words and phrases to push their own spiritual agenda, New Age leaders like Marianne Williamson quote King phrases like "beloved community,"[3] "a new dimension of love,"[4] spiritually "one,"[5] and "the birth of a new age,"[6] in their effort to use King's "dream" of eliminating racism to float their own dream—"God's Dream." But there is nothing in King's writings, speeches, or on the Internet to indicate that the Baptist preacher ever used the term "God's Dream" or would endorse their New Age/New Gospel/New Spirituality.

With a willingness to pull out-of-context phrases from King's speeches and writings—even from youthful and idealistic college essays—it seems that New Age leaders want everyone to believe Martin Luther King Jr. was really a closet New Ager—a New Age prophet far ahead of his time. It seems they think that if King were alive today, he would be the first to champion their "civil rights movement for the soul." But this is simply not true. King believed in the sinfulness of man, not in the divinity of man.

In a 2002 *Unitarian Universalist World* magazine article, Unitarian minister Rosemary Bray McNatt addressed the subject of why Martin Luther King was *not* a Unitarian Universalist.[7] She cited King's famous essay, "Pilgrimage to Non-Violence" where King clarified that his liberal theology only went so far. He said:

> It was . . . the liberal doctrine of man that I began to question. The more I observed the tragedies of history, and man's shameful inclination to choose the low road, the more I came to see the depths and strengths of sin. . . . I came to feel that liberalism had been all too sentimental concerning human nature and that it leaned toward a false idealism. I also came to see that liberalism's superficial optimism concerning human nature caused it to overlook the fact that reason is darkened by sin.[8]

King's ardent plea for a "beloved community" and "the birth of a new age" was always in regard to civil rights and racial equality—it was never to promote a New Age/New Spirituality that teaches God is "in" everyone and everything. His hope for a "new order"/"new world order"[9] and in people becoming spiritually "one"[10] was aimed at abolishing racism—not in establishing a New Age/New World Religion.

Trying to Link MLK to God's Dream

In short, "God's Dream" is a cunningly devised spiritual trap that uses Martin Luther King's person and message to bring occult teachings into the world and into the church. Given the New Age push for "God's Dream" and a "God's Dream" Peace Plan, an important question needs to be asked—"Why are so many Christian leaders using this same New Age concept of "God's Dream" as they similarly equate it to Martin Luther King and his "I have a dream" speech? For example, controversial emergent author and former pastor Brian McLaren writes:

> For all these reasons, "the dream of God" strikes me as a beautiful way to translate the message of the kingdom of God for hearers today. It is, of course, the language evoked by Martin Luther King Jr. as he stood on the steps of the Lincoln Memorial on August 28, 1963. His dream was God's dream, and that accounted for its amazing power.[11]

Lou Engle, the founder of the ministry, The Call, delivered a highly charged "God's Dream" speech in 2008 to thousands of youth gathered at the Washington Mall. He proclaimed:

> Forty years ago this year, Martin Luther King sounded a prophetic trumpet to the nation. . . . Gathering at the mall in Washington D.C. the sound was born of "I have a dream" and that same sound still resonates today. Today, the sound is being carried across the pulpits of the pews of America, extending from the senatorial chambers of Washington D.C. to the movie industry of Hollywood. It is the sound of another great movement on the horizon, a prayer and justice movement crying out for God's dreams to be fulfilled in a generation.[12]

In a preacher's commentary written by David McKenna and edited by the late former pastor and senate chaplain Lloyd Ogilvie, we find this same effort to link the concept of "God's Dream" with Martin Luther King:

> Martin Luther King is best known for his speech, "I Have a Dream." He dreamed of equality of the races and social justice for all people. The Book of Isaiah might be read as God saying, "I Have a Dream." If so, we would see that God dreamed of a future in which righteousness prevailed among the people and peace prevailed among the nations.[13]

The accelerated use of the term "God's Dream" within the church—particularly in relation to Martin Luther King—seems to spiritually legitimize what is, in effect, an antichrist, New Age concept. What is being missed by most Christians—especially Christian leaders—is that in New Age circles, "God's Dream" has already become a spiritual device that is paving the way for a false Christ and a New World Religion.

Brief History of "God's Dream"

God's Dream and the New Age

It is important to remember that the term "God's Dream" can be traced at least as far back as the early 1900s where it was referenced in two theosophical/occult magazines published for those interested in Theosophy and the future coming of their "Christ," Maitreya. "God's Dream" was the title of a poem that introduced an article titled "Practical Theosophy" in a 1904 issue of *New Century Path* magazine.[14] Twelve years later, the term "God's Dream" appeared again in a February 1916 issue of *The Theosophical Path* magazine.[15]

The Encyclopedia Britannica notes that the occultism that eventually came to be known as the New Age movement in the 1970s and

1980s, had its origins in those early British theosophical groups. The encyclopedia said:

> The international New Age movement of the 1970s and '80s originated among independent theosophical groups in the United Kingdom.[16]

Most people in today's church are not aware of the occult/New Age origin of the term "God's Dream" from the early 1900s and how it has been used by a wide variety of New Age figures ever since. Here are some selected examples.

***The Theosophical Path* magazine (1916)**—The following quote is from the February 1916 issue of *The Theosophical Path* magazine:

> We shall think then that this Earth and all her bright companions in the vast space are but drops of joy solidified, and the intense wonder and beauty of God's dream.[17]

Paramahansa Yogananda (1945)—This popular Eastern guru and yogi came to America and established a spiritual center in Southern California called the Self-Realization Fellowship (SRF). His book *Autobiography of a Yogi* has been a perennial best-seller. Paramahansa Yogananda spent his last thirty years in the United States and was responsible for teaching millions of Americans how to meditate and practice Yoga. He consistently taught about the alleged unity of Eastern and Western religions and would periodically reference "God's Dream" in his talks and writings. In a 1945 talk at his Self-Realization Fellowship Temple in Hollywood, California, Yogananda stated:

> That is the philosophy the great masters of India teach— that this world, this creation, is the dream of God.[18]

Sri Chinmoy (1974)—The late United Nations resident guru, Sri Chinmoy, conducted New Age meditations at the U.N. and had close associations with Mikhail Gorbachev, Nelson Mandela, and other world leaders. He said:

> God's Dream-Boat is man. . . .

> When you become one with God, you see that everything in God's Dream already embodies the Reality itself.[19]

The "Jesus" of *A Course in Miracles* (1975)—Just as the false Christ Maitreya channeled the concept of "God's Dream" through Benjamin Creme, "God's Dream" and *A Course in Miracles* was similarly channeled—allegedly by "Jesus"—through a psychologist in New York City named Helen Schucman. In fact, "God's Dream" is the foundational concept of these *Course* channelings that were published in 1975 as *A Course in Miracles*. This New Age *Course* was popularized by psychiatrist Gerald Jampolsky's 1979 book *Love is Letting Go of Fear* and New Age author Marianne Williamson's 1992 book *A Return to Love: Reflections on the Principles of A Course in Miracles*. Oprah Winfrey publicly promoted Williamson's book, and through her enthusiastic endorsement almost single-handedly made it a #1 *New York Times* best-seller. In hyping Williamson's book on the *Course*, Oprah said the teachings of *A Course in Miracles* "could change the world"[20]—New Age teachings that were all based on the concept of "God's Dream."

The whole philosophy of *A Course in Miracles* boils down to this same basic New Age teaching of Oneness versus Separation. The *Course's* New Age "Jesus" teaches that "The oneness of the Creator and the creation is your wholeness, your sanity and your limitless power."[21] Because all is alleged to be love and because God is love, all is therefore God, and all is therefore "One." Thus, because all is God, and all is "One," the *Course* falsely teaches that "[t]here is no separation of God and His creation."[22] Believing that we are "separate" from God—that all is not God and all is not "One"—is described by the *Course's* "Jesus" as a "sickness,"[23] an "illusion,"[24] and the "devil."[25]

The *Course* teaches that "[a] sense of separation from God is the only lack you really need correct."[26] And how is this sense of separation corrected? It is corrected by "God's Dream." *A Course in Miracles'* "Jesus" teaches that because all fear is delusional and part of a hapless dream, we, as dreamers, need to be gently wakened from our hapless dreams by God's "happy dreams."[27] To deliver us from our hapless dreams, we are told by the *Course's* "Jesus" that God is now sending us his dreams—"God's Dreams"—to wake us up to the self-realization that "we are all one" because "we are all love" because "we are all God." Referring to "God's Dream" for us, the *Course's* "Jesus" states:

> Accept the dream He gave instead of yours. It is not diffi-cult to change a dream when once the dreamer has been recognized. Rest in the Holy Spirit, and allow His gentle dreams to take the place of those you dreamed in terror and in fear of death.[28]

In a talk with the Robert Schulleresque title—"God Will Re-deem His Dream"—New Apostolic Reformation (NAR) "apostle" Dutch Sheets sounds just like the counterfeit "Jesus" of *A Course in Miracles* regarding "God's Dream" when he says:

> That's the way God works. He gives you a dream but he hides a dream of his in your dream.[29]

Unbelievably, New Age *A Course in Miracles* study groups, led by a Robert Schuller staff member, met in classrooms at Robert Schuller's Crystal Cathedral in the mid-1980s.[30] During this same time that they were meeting, pastors and church leaders from the U.S. and around the world were attending Schuller's Institute for Successful Church Leadership on the same cathedral grounds. But those attending didn't seem too concerned about Schuller's obvious New Age sympathies. They were too busy studying Schuller's "dare to dream" "God's Dream" success strategies on how to make their churches bigger and better and more successful.

The late psychiatrist Dr. Gerald Jampolsky was chief spokesperson for *A Course in Miracles* for five decades—just as Oprah Winfrey and author Marianne Williamson have publicly promoted the *Course* for over three decades. What becomes obvious is that the *Course's* "God's Dream" teachings on Oneness vs. Separation provide the spiritual groundwork for a New Age/New Gospel/New Spirituality that was specifically designed to eliminate and replace the foundational teachings of biblical Christianity.

Sun Myung Moon (1978)—Claiming to be the second coming of Christ, the late Sun Myung Moon was the false Christ leader of the "Moonies" and their worldwide Unification Church. His description of "God's Dream" is very similar to references in both the New Age movement and the NAR of today's professing church. In a 1978 talk, he stated:

> God's dream still remains unfulfilled. It was not fulfilled 2,000 years ago, or in the home of any religious leader or any American home, and today the Unification Church is here to pledge to fulfill that dream. We don't want to confine that fulfillment to our Church, but to expand it all over the world. Wouldn't that be the Kingdom of God on earth?[31]

Maitreya (1980)—The false Christ Maitreya claims to be here in our world waiting for humanity to call him forth. In his 1980 channeled book, *Messages from Maitreya the Christ*, he reinforced the 1916 *The Theosophical Path* magazine article referencing "God's Dream." He stated:

> I am with you as God's Representative, as the Spokesman
> for that Divine Being Whose dreams we are.[32]

Wayne Dyer (1989)—The late best-selling author and psychologist, Wayne Dyer, was a familiar figure on Public Television (PBS) as he presented his New Age take on things. In his 1989 book *You'll See It When You Believe It*, he stated:

> Who is the ultimate dreamer? Call it as you will: God, higher consciousness, Krishna, Spirit, whatever pleases you. . . .
>
> One dream, one dreamer, billions of embodied characters setting out that one dream . . . Your true essence is that you are part and parcel of the one big dream.
>
> You the dreamer . . . God the dreamer.[33]

Neale Donald Walsch (2008)—This New Age author has had a series of best-selling books and writings based on his alleged "conversations with God" on a variety of subjects, including "God's Dream." As cited, in a 2008 online message, he wrote:

> God's "dream," if you please, is that we will all one day be completely realized [as "God"].[34]

Oprah Winfrey (2016)—At a 2006 "Live Your Best Life" seminar, Oprah used the term "God's Dream." She said:

> I live inside God's dream for me. . . . God can dream a bigger dream for you than you can dream for yourself.[35]

She also talked about "God's Dream" at the 2016 Essence Festival in New Orleans. She asked those gathered:

What is God's Dream for you? . . . The key, the secret, the magic is to surrender to God's Dream for you.[36]

God's Dream and the Church

As mentioned, when "God's Dream" is searched on the Internet, there are countless Christian references to this key New Age phrase. However, it is never—not even once—brought up in Scripture. What becomes apparent is that this century-old New Age concept has become an overlapping term to unify the world and the church through a mutually shared dream—"God's Dream." However, because the term "God's Dream" has no biblical justification and is clearly a New Age device, we must ask the obvious question—"How did the century-old theosophical New Age concept of "God's Dream" ever enter the church?"

The New Age concept of "God's Dream" was brought into the church as early as 1974 by the late Robert Schuller. It was reintroduced, reinforced, and highly popularized by pastor Rick Warren in 2003—and on up to the present. Thanks to Schuller and Warren, "God's Dream" has become a go-to metaphor in today's church. The following is just a small sampling of how this overlapping term has entered the church and continues to be a falsely unifying metaphor.

Robert Schuller (1974)—The late Robert Schuller introduced the term "God's Dream" in his 1974 book *Your Church Has Real Possibilities*. He wrote:

Now pray the prayer of surrender. . . . Then ask the Holy Spirit to fill your mind with God's dream for your life.[37]

He also used the term "God's Dream" in his 1978 book *Discover Your Possibilities*:

Pray, seek God's guidance and what's going to happen? You'll get a dream to pursue. . . . Find a dream. Once you've got that dream and you know it's God's dream for your life, then be daring. Dare to say it. Let the redeemed of the Lord say so. Announce to the whole world that it's going to happen.[38]

Schuller continued to lay the groundwork for "God's Dream" by elaborating on the concept in his 1982 book *Self-Esteem: The New Reformation*. He used the term in a number of different contexts. He wrote:

> When God's dream is accepted, we must be prepared to pay a high price.[39]

> I am not fully forgiven until I allow God to write his new dream for my life on the blackboard of my mind, and I dare to believe "I am; therefore, I can. I am a child of God. I am somebody. God has a great plan to redeem society. He needs me and wants to use me."[40]

> Tremendous human energy is needed to walk God's walk, work God's work, fulfill God's will, and complete his dream for our self-esteem.[41]

Robert Schuller continued to use and popularize the term "God's Dream" up to the time of his death in 2015. In fact, one of the last books he wrote was titled *Don't Throw Away Tomorrow: Living God's Dream for Your Life.*

Rick Warren (2003)—In an October 27, 2003 e-mail to his church titled "God's Dream for You—And the World!," Rick Warren introduced "God's Dream" as being at the heart of his "New Reformation" Global Peace Plan. Some two decades after Robert Schuller introduced "God's Dream" as being at the heart of *his* "New Reformation" plan to "redeem society," Rick Warren effectively re-presented a more detailed version of Schuller's original plan.

Following Schuller's 1978 instruction to "Announce to the whole world" that "God's Dream" is "going to happen," Rick Warren said the very same thing. He presented "God's Dream" for the church and the world and used Schuller's own words to reaffirm that "God's Dream" "is going to happen." He also said that his "God's Dream" "Global P.E.A.C.E. Plan" would "bring worldwide revival"[42] and "change history." In this 2003 e-mail to his church to be shared with the world, Rick Warren headlined it with "God's Dream" and wrote the following:

GOD'S DREAM FOR YOU—AND THE WORLD!

> THIS WEEKEND, I'll begin a series of five messages on God's dream to use you globally—to literally use YOU to help change the world! I'll unveil our Global P.E.A.C.E. plan, and how God has uniquely prepared you for this moment of destiny. . . .

> God is going to use you, and all of us together at Saddleback, to change history! . . .

> The Global Peace Plan IS GOING TO HAPPEN.[43]

Over the years, Rick Warren has continued to popularize this overlapping New Age concept of "God's Dream." It is found in many of his sermons, writings, radio programs, and videos. In the process, he has passed the concept of "God Dream" on to countless pastors and church leaders who trust him and look to him for leadership.

In 2016, Rick Warren presented a six-part sermon series on DVD titled *God's Dream for Your Life*. The title is the exact subtitle of Robert Schuller's 2005 book *Don't Throw Away Tomorrow: God's Dream for Your Life*. A Rick Warren article titled, "How You Can Realize God's Dream for Your Life" was also published in a 2016 issue of *Charisma* magazine.[44] In a 2016 *Daily Hope* "devotional" piece titled "Dream Big," Rick Warren used Robert Schuller's 1978 "dare to dream God's Dream" concept. He wrote that in order to receive God's blessing, you "must dare to ask . . . God, what's your dream for my life?" He went so far as to suggest that one's faith is dependent on "choosing and believing God's dream for your life." In that devotional piece, he wrote:

> If you want God's blessing on your life this year, you must dare to ask for it. You must say, "God, what's your dream for my life?"[45]

> Faith is choosing and believing God's dream for your life. Nothing starts happening in your life until you start dreaming.[46]

Beginning in February 2020, Rick Warren initiated a 40-day "spiritual growth campaign" titled "Time to Dream" that again focused on the concept of "God's Dream." In a sermon titled "Dreaming the Future God Wants for You," Warren stated:

> If you don't dream you are sinning.[47]

The accompanying sermon notes said:

> After your relationship with Jesus, knowing God's dream for your life is the second-most important thing you will ever discover.[48]

Bruce Wilkinson (2003)—In October 2003, one of Rick Warren's self-described "best friends in the whole world," Bruce Wilkinson,[49] came to Saddleback to preach for a whole week about various aspects of "God's Dream." His messages, along with his new book *The Dream Giver*, were perfectly timed and designed to set the stage for Rick Warren's announcement about "God's Dream"—his

Global P.E.A.C.E. Plan for the church and the world. In one of his many references to "God's Dream" in *The Dream Giver*, Wilkinson wrote:

> You have been handcrafted by God to accomplish a part of His Big Dream for the world.[50]

Sarah Young (2004)—*Jesus Calling* author Sarah Young claimed that she received direct messages from "Jesus" Himself. She wrote them down and turned them into numerous best-selling "Christian" books. In 2004 in *Jesus Calling*, her "Jesus" says:

> I may infuse within you a dream that seems far beyond your reach.[51]

The concept of "God's Dream" was also included in her 2010 book for children titled *Jesus Calling: 365 Devotions for Kids*. Her "Jesus" states:

> Dream your biggest, most incredible dream—and then know that I am able to do far more than that, far more than you can ever ask or imagine. Allow Me to fill your mind with My dreams for you.[52]

Brian McLaren (2006)—In his 2006 book *The Secret Message of Jesus*, controversial church figure and former pastor Brian McLaren writes:

> The call to faith is the call to trust God and God's dreams enough to realign our dreams with God's, to dream our little dreams within God's big dream.[53]

As previously cited, McLaren juxtaposes the concept of "God's Dream" with Martin Luther King's famous "I have a dream" speech—even though King never used the term "God's Dream" in his writings. McLaren writes:

> For all these reasons, "the dream of God" strikes me as a beautiful way to translate the message of the kingdom of God for hearers today. It is, of course, the language evoked by Dr. Martin Luther King Jr. as he stood on the steps of the Lincoln Memorial on August 28, 1963. His dream was God's dream, and that accounted for its amazing power.[54]

Shane Claiborne (2008)—In his 2008 book *Jesus for President*, this emergent author and social activist states:

> The end of war begins with people who believe that another world is possible and that another empire has already interrupted time and space and is taking over this earth with the dreams of God.[55]

Ravi Zacharias (2008)—The late Ravi Zacharias highlighted his 2008 National Day of Prayer keynote address in Washington D.C. by referring to "God's Dream," stating:

> You're the dream of God. He fashions you into his dream.[56]

Ten years later in 2018, speaking to 300 pastors and church leaders at a National Day of Prayer event honoring them, Zacharias again stressed the concept of "God's Dream" when he said:

> Prayer is what takes place when God is making you His dream. I think to me God was unfolding His dream in my life as He was unfolding it for a whole nation.[57]

Jim Wallis (2016)—In 2016, social-justice activist Jim Wallis stated that "God's dream" will "shape the end of human history." He wrote:

> We are still very much in the midst of the fulfillment of God's dream, but it is deeply satisfying that, even in the face of our pain and struggle, we have seen that dream and believe it will shape the end of human history.[58]

Joel Osteen (2017)—On a March 11, 2017 YouTube video, Houston Lakewood Church pastor Joel Osteen delivered a sermon titled "God's Dream for Your Life Is to Be Blessed and Be a Blessing to Others." In a July 2014 daily devotional titled "God's Dream for Your Life," Osteen stated:

> God's dream for your life is much bigger than your own.[59]

Pope Francis (2018)—Pope Francis frequently uses the term "God's Dream." He has stated:

> God's "dream" is his people.[60]

> God wants us to be able to dream like he does and, with him as we journey, to be quite attentive to reality—dreaming of a different world.[61]

> We are the dream of God who, truly in love, wants to change our life through love.[62]

Dr. Alan Keyes (2020)—In a June 9, 2020 article posted at ChurchMilitant.com and titled "God's Dream Is Better for Us," conservative Catholic political reformer, Alan Keyes, expressed his thoughts about the death of George Floyd and the massive protests that ensued. Joining the popular chorus of those equating "God's Dream" with Martin Luther King's "dream," Keyes presented

"God's dream" as the positive antidote for America's social, political, and racial unrest. Invoking "God's Dream," Keyes wrote:

> Like MLK, America has a dream. These deluded self-made gods have only a nightmare. Whatever our faults, Americans must never forget: God's dream for us is better. Let us open our eyes to Him and let it be.[63]

The term "God's Dream" has also been used by Chip Ingram,[64] Mark Batterson,[65] James Robison,[66] Sally Lloyd-Jones,[67] Kenneth Copeland[68] and many other church figures. Because the concept of "God's Dream" was so heavily championed by Robert Schuller and Rick Warren over the years, this overlapping New Age term is now deeply embedded in today's professing church. It has come a long way from those obscure references in New Age theosophical magazines over a century ago.

"God's Dream" and Revival

A question that necessarily arises is: Why are so many Christian leaders using a term like "God's Dream" that has no biblical precedent or scriptural justification? The answer is because they have unwittingly adopted an overlapping New Age term brought into the church and popularized by Robert Schuller and Rick Warren. "God's Dream" is now being used to characterize, encourage, and bring to fruition a "great awakening," a "great worldwide revival." The following are some of the ways this "God's Dream" "revival" is being presented by today's church leaders and how they say it will allegedly change and fulfill "history."

Leonard Sweet (1999)—Church leader Leonard Sweet described this future world "revival" as the fulfillment of "God's Dream."

In his 1999 book *soulTsunami*, he says it is "a race to the future" and that we all have to "save God's Dream":

> There is a race to the future. Who will get there first? Will the Christian church? The time to save God's Dream is now. The people to save God's Dream are you. . . .
> God is birthing the greatest spiritual awakening in the history of the church. God is calling you to midwife that birth. Are you going to show up?[69]

Rick Warren (2003)—As previously cited, Saddleback pastor Rick Warren introduced his Global Peace Plan in 2003 as "God's Dream for You—And the World!" and how it would "change history." One of his former apologists stated that one of Warren's purposes regarding his "God's Dream" Peace Plan is to "bring worldwide revival."[70]

Bill Johnson (2006)—In his 2006 book *Dreaming With God*, NAR Bethel Church pastor Bill Johnson writes:

> Learning the dreams of God for this world is our beginning place.[71]

> I write that His Church would rise to her potential and change the course of world history.[72]

Lou Engle (2008)—In 2008, NAR leader Lou Engle called for the "dreamers of God's dream" to be "history-makers." A video once posted on Engle's website showed a stadium full of young people with a Scripture marked on their foreheads. A concerned writer noted:

> A highly disturbing video posted at The Call's website describes the extreme nature of this youth movement,

and states that "those who come will be marked forever and they will be history-makers and dreamers of God's dream.[73]

In fact, the day-to-day heading on revivalist Lou Engle's 2023 website features the concept of "God's Dream." It states:

> When God created you, he had a dream and wrapped a body around that dream to fulfill it.[74]

Right below this is the big bold statement:

HISTORY IN THE MAKING."[75]

Lou Engle was featured with Bill Johnson, Rodney Howard-Browne, Benny Hinn, Todd White, Francis Chan, and other church figures in a 2019 "The Send" Conference led by NAR leaders to give further impetus to their much heralded "God's Dream" revival—their "Great Spiritual Awakening." In promoting 2023 revival events, Engle states on his website:

> We dare to believe that God is restoring lost biblical truths while also releasing fresh, new revelations to the church.[76]

What Lou Engle is saying is exactly what New Age leaders are saying—that we need to recover lost truths and we need new revelation.

Sean Feucht (2020)—Echoing Lou Engle, Sean Feucht, a "revivalist" with a recent history as a worship leader at Bill Johnson's Bethel Church, writes:

> [A] company of people exists in almost every city. . . . They are the dreamers. They are the history makers.[77]

Feucht, having been greatly influenced by Lou Engle, is the founder of Burn 24/7, a "revival" movement in which its "heartbeat" is rooted in the concept of "God's Dream"—"to see the Father's dream for this generation realized."[78] On Feucht's *Burn 24/7* website, under core values, it states:

We can become the dream of God.[79]

Deception, Not Revival

The New Age concept of "God's Dream" has been in the world for well over a century. But God doesn't dream, daydream, or pipedream when it comes to the future. God already knows the future and what it holds. Thankfully, He has warned us about it ahead of time in Scripture. Instead of a coming great revival, He has warned about a coming great deception. He says this deception will come through false Christs, false prophets, false teachers, false signs and wonders, and a false peace that is orchestrated by our spiritual Adversary. And He specifically warns us to beware of "filthy dreamers" (Jude 1:8) and "dreamer[s] of dreams" (Deuteronomy 13:1-3) who prophesy "false dreams" like "God's Dream," that have nothing to do with Him.

Behold, I am against them that prophesy false dreams, saith the LORD, and do tell them, and cause my people to err by their lies, and by their lightness; yet I sent them not, nor commanded them: therefore they shall not profit this people at all, saith the LORD. (Jeremiah 23:32)

Keep that which is committed to thy trust,
avoiding profane and vain babblings,
and oppositions of science falsely so
called: Which some professing have erred
concerning the faith. (1 Timothy 6:20-21)

Quantum Spirituality–
Science Falsely So Called

Leonard Sweet–A Quantum Spirituality Pioneer

Leonard Sweet is an ordained Methodist minister who is the E. Stanley Jones Emeritus Professor of Evangelism at Drew University in Madison, New Jersey. He is also a visiting distinguished professor at George Fox University in Portland, Oregon, and he is one of the co-founders of the huge Global Church Network. On his website, he is described as a "scholar of American culture" who has authored over 70 books and countless articles and has published over 1500 sermons.[1] A Phi Beta Kappa graduate, he frequently speaks at conferences around the world and "serves as a consultant to many of America's denominational leaders and agencies." Descriptive terms such as "distinguished," "most influential," "widely quoted," "highly sought after," and "the Picasso of Preaching" give visitors to his website the distinct impression that this is a man they should definitely pay attention to. And many people are doing just that.

Day-to-day believers may or may not be familiar with Leonard Sweet, but many in Christian leadership are *very* familiar with this self-described "semiotician." According to his website, a semiotician is someone who "sees things the rest of us do not see and dreams possibilities that are beyond most of our imagining." And as a "cultural futurist" and "Christ follower," he seems to be very comfortable assuming the role of a postmodern prophet who provides hip observations of what is and what will be. His mission is to help the church become more culturally relevant in the 21st century. However, as he attempts to walk the narrow line between the Gospel and the world, he frequently walks over that line into the false teachings of the New Age/New Gospel/New Spirituality. When he does, legitimate questions need to be raised about what he is doing.

In June 2010, Leonard Sweet became the object of a swirling controversy, and his name suddenly disappeared from the list of scheduled speakers at a National Worship Conference taking place in Albuquerque, New Mexico. The controversy centered around the New Age implications of many of the quotes and teachings found in his 1991 book *Quantum Spirituality: A Postmodern Apologetic*. Prior to the conference, a number of people were starting to ask obvious questions about Sweet and what he was conveying. In *A "Wonderful" Deception*, I wrote three chapters on Leonard Sweet and the obvious New Age implications of what he was teaching. In the first chapter on Sweet, I described some of my initial impressions regarding this man, and in particular, his book *Quantum Spirituality*. I wrote:

> Highly intellectual and well-read, Leonard Sweet almost dares you to keep up with him as he charges through the spiritual marketplace. Operating at lightning speed and quoting from countless books and articles, he will impress many readers with his quick wit and spiritual insights. However, as he treacherously dives into New Age waters and challenges his readers to go there with him, serious problems arise within his "postmodern apologetic."

In reading *Quantum Spirituality*, I recalled the Sermon on the Mount when Jesus warned that you can't serve two masters (Matthew 6:24). Leonard Sweet may be a professing evangelical Christian, but he also simultaneously praises New Age authors and their teachings.[2]

Sweet's "Response" to Critics

Keenly aware of the controversy he has created, Sweet has a statement posted on the blog of his home website titled—"A Response to Recent Misunderstandings." While his attempt to explain himself might satisfy the uninformed reader, his "Response" does not address the specifics of what he has written and is actually teaching. His simplistic denunciation of the New Age is unconvincing. His statement that the "New Age rhymes with sewage" and his encouraging the use of a "daily ritual of starting the day by standing in front of a mirror and saying: "God is God and I am not" do not speak to the fact that he has never addressed, much less renounced, the specific New Age teachings that he was otherwise appearing to deny and disparage. And his stating "back when the New Age was a movement" completely misses the fact that the New Age movement never went away. Those of us who came out of New Age teachings and have been observing the New Age over the past several decades know that contrary to Sweet's claims, the New Age movement has actually grown exponentially and is now mainstream and an inherent part of our culture. Due to its continued wide-spread growth and influence, the New Age threat to the church (and the world) is larger than ever before. But now it is just hiding in plain sight behind the facade of other names like "New Spirituality," "New Gospel," "New Worldview," or in Sweet's case—the "New Light" teachings of a "quantum spirituality."

Because Sweet's "A Response to Recent Misunderstandings" left so many unanswered questions and because of his continued influence in the church, it seems imperative that thoughtful

Christians take a deeper look at what Leonard Sweet is *really* teaching. For starters, here are five immediate concerns to consider.

Five Immediate Concerns

I. Leonard Sweet teaches the New Age doctrine of "Immanence" that would have the church believe God is "in" everyone and everything.

In her 1948 book *The Reappearance of the Christ,* New Age matriarch Alice Bailey and her spirit guide Djwhal Khul describe how the path to their New Age God will be based on an "immanent" God that is "within every form of life":

> . . . a fresh orientation to divinity and to the acceptance of the fact of God Transcendent and of *God Immanent within every form of life.* These are the foundational truths upon which the world religion of the future will rest.[3] (emphasis added)

Likewise, in his 1980 book, *The Reappearance of the Christ and the Masters of Wisdom,* New Age channeler Benjamin Creme, states that the New World Religion will be based on the proposition that "Christ" is "immanent"—"in man and all creation":

> But eventually a new world religion will be inaugurated which will be a fusion and synthesis of the approach of the East and the approach of the West. The Christ will bring together, not simply Christianity and Buddhism, but the concept of God transcendent—outside of His creation—and also the concept of *God immanent in all creation—in man and all creation.*[4] (emphasis added)

In Leonard Sweet's 1999 book *soulTsunami*—with its front cover endorsement by Rick Warren—Sweet introduces this same

New Age idea of God not only being transcendent but also immanent. He wrote:

> To survive in postmodern culture, one has to learn to speak out of both sides of the mouth. It should not be hard, since Christianity has always insisted on having things both ways. Isn't it based on the impossible possibility of Jesus being "beyond us, yet ourselves" (poet Wallace Stevens)? Biblical theological is not circular with a fixed center, but elliptical, revolving around the double foci of God's *immanence* and God's transcendence.[5] (emphasis added)

Sweet clearly spells out what he means by "immanence" in his book *Quantum Spirituality: A Postmodern Apologetic*. As a self-described "radical," he presents his "radical doctrine" that God is immanently embodied "in" His creation. He writes:

> Quantum spirituality bonds us to all creation as well as to other members of the human family. . . . This entails *a radical doctrine of embodiment of God in the very substance of creation*. . . . But a spirituality that is not in some way entheistic (whether pan- or trans-), that does not extend to the *spirit-matter* of the cosmos, is not Christian.[6] (emphasis added)

But Sweet's "radical" panentheistic doctrine is a key New Age teaching—as is so much of what he wrote in *Quantum Spirituality*. In his "A Response to Recent Misunderstandings," Sweet tries to dispel questions about quantum spirituality by saying, "Would I write the same book today? No. Would I say the same things differently? Yes. I started working on the book in my late 20s. I hope I'm older and wiser now." However, when it comes to the New Age implications of what he is teaching, he is *not* any wiser in regard to his previously stated New Age doctrine. In several subsequent books, Sweet reintroduces his New Age doctrine of immanence—that God is immanently embodied "in" His creation. For example, in *soulTsunami,* he wrote:

> Postmodern evangelism is first of all telling people how special they are, how much God loves them, how unique each and every one of them is. The fourth-century theologian Athanasius said in one of his letters that God became one of us "that he might deify us in Himself." Similarly, elsewhere he wrote that Christ "was made man that we might be made God."[7]

In Sweet's 2010 book *Nudge: Awakening Each Other to the God Who's Already There,* he expresses in different words what he wrote in *Quantum Spirituality* about the "embodiment of God in the very substance of creation":

> An incarnational God means that God-stuff is found in the matter of the universe.[8]

In *Nudge* he also wrote, "Nudgers help people discover their inner Jesus."[9] But God is not "in" everyone and everything and Jesus is not "in" everyone and everything. Sweet may *seem* to denounce the New Age, but what he is teaching *is* New Age. This is dangerous and unbiblical leaven. The apostle Paul lamented that it only took "a little leaven" to lure the Galatians away from the Gospel they once knew so well. He wrote:

> Ye did run well; who did hinder you that ye should not obey the truth? This persuasion cometh not of him that calleth you. A little leaven leaveneth the whole lump. (Galatians 5:7-9)

God states in the first commandment, "Thou shalt have no other gods before me." The New Age "God" who is "in" everyone and everything is another "God" and therefore a false God. Contrary to Leonard Sweet's teaching in *Quantum Spirituality,* God is *not* embodied in His creation. Contrary to his teaching in *Nudge,* "God-stuff" is *not* found in the matter of the universe, and everyone does not have an "inner Jesus." Scripture is very clear. Man is not God because God is not "in" everyone and everything. In Jeremiah 16:20, God warned: "Shall a man make gods unto himself, and they are no gods?" In Matthew 23:12, Jesus warned, "And whosoever shall exalt himself shall be abased; and he that shall humble himself shall be exalted."

II. Leonard Sweet describes the "Father" of the New Age movement as "Twentieth-century Christianity's major voice."
Sweet describes heretical Jesuit Catholic priest Pierre Teilhard de Chardin—the "Father" of the New Age movement—as "Twentieth-century Christianity's major voice."[10] In her best-selling New Age classic, *The Aquarian Conspiracy,* author Marilyn Ferguson describes Teilhard de Chardin as "the individual most often named as a profound influence by the aquarian conspirators who responded to a survey."[11] He is also the most frequently referenced New Age leader in her book. The Teilhard quote "This soul can only be a conspiracy of individuals" is found on the very first page of her book and inspired her to title her book *The Aquarian Conspiracy.* Ferguson wrote that "Teilhard prophesied the phenomenon central to this book: a conspiracy of men and women whose new perspective would trigger a critical contagion of change."[12]

Evident in his posted "Response," Sweet appears to be baffled by everyone's concern about some of the things he is writing. He seems to take any criticism as a personal attack. But this criticism, if you will, is not about him personally, it is about what he is teaching. Jesus didn't say "Get thee behind me, Satan" to Peter because he thought Peter was Satan. He said "Get thee behind me, Satan" because of what Peter was *saying.* And because Sweet is saying the "Father" of the New Age movement is "Twentieth-century

Christianity's major voice," we need to look at what Teilhard is teaching about the Christian faith. The following unbiblical statements were made by Teilhard de Chardin in his book *Christianity and Evolution*. He wrote:

> The cross still stands . . . But this is on one condition, and one only, that it expand itself to the dimensions of a *New Age*, and cease to present itself to us as primarily (or even exclusively) the sign of a victory over sin.[13]

> What I am proposing to do is to narrow that gap between pantheism and Christianity by bringing out what one might call *the Christian soul of pantheism* or *the pantheistic aspect of Christianity*.[14]

> I can be saved only by *becoming one* with the universe.[15]

> I believe that the Messiah whom we await, whom we all without any doubt await, is the *universal Christ*; that is to say, the Christ of evolution.[16]

> [I]f a Christ is to be completely acceptable as an object of worship, he must be presented as the saviour of the idea and reality of *evolution*.[17]

> A general convergence of religions upon a *universal Christ* who fundamentally satisfies them all: that seems to me the only possible conversion of the world, and the only form in which a religion of the future can be conceived.[18]

> (italics added for emphasis on all of the above quotes)

Teilhard Again?

Sweet's affection for Teilhard de Chardin surfaced again in his 1999 book *Aqua Church*. After quoting a strong Bible-based stanza from the hymn "Jesus Savior Pilot Me," Sweet follows it by positively quoting Teilhard de Chardin. Teilhard stated that those who "see" Christ as he does, understand Christ in "a much more magnificent way" than all those who went before him:

> Christ is in the Church in the same way as the sun is before our eyes. We see the same sun as our fathers saw, and yet we understand it in a much more magnificent way.[19]

Really? Teilhard and his followers understand Christ in a much more magnificent way than all the previous believers throughout the centuries? More than all the martyrs? More than the original disciples? This seems to indicate that Teilhard and Sweet and their "semiotic" emergent postmodern "Christ followers" are "seeing" something about Christ that the rest of the church does not see. Would Sweet have the church believe that Chardin's seemingly updated New Age "Christ" is the *real* Christ? Is the "semiotic" Sweet trying to show us that if we adopt the New Age teachings of Teilhard, we, too, will "see" Christ in a "much more magnificent way" than the Christians who came before us? Sadly, it would seem that this is so.

Sweet seems to believe that with new understandings from quantum physics, a New Age/New Gospel/New Spirituality/quantum spirituality would enable Christians to see Christ in a much deeper and "more magnificent way." The church would finally understand that the science of quantum physics is "proving" that God is an energy force that interpenetrates and embodies His creation. Therefore, we are all "connected" because we are all "God" because God is "in" everyone and everything. Sweet argues that Christians of the past weren't ready to deal with things like quantum physics, quantum wavelengths, and the New Age implications of a quantum spirituality that would totally transform their faith and challenge everything they thought they knew about being a Christian. In his 2016 book *Jesus Speaks*, Leonard Sweet wrote:

> The Holy Spirit brings Jesus' voice to life through history, theology, science, and social experience. Jesus told the disciples, "I have much more to say to you" (John 16:12). In other words, Jesus was saying, "You can't handle everything I have to say to you right now. Some of my truth has a wavelength, and it needs time, maybe even centuries, to play itself out.[20]

But this implies that God's Word is incomplete and insufficient and therefore in need of "new truth" and "new revelation." This is simply not true. Besides, when Jesus said "I have much more to say to you, He was talking to His disciples—not to the church today. It is also important to notice how Sweet conveniently squeezed "wavelength" into his interpretation of Jesus' words to set up his quantum spirituality. But Jesus wasn't withholding spiritual insights that would have to be delivered to His people two thousand years later. This kind of false teaching is an inherent part of the New Age deception. The fact is Jesus has already given us everything we need to know in His Holy Bible.

Jesus warned of false prophets who would come in sheep's clothing (Matthew 7:15). And that there would be those who honor Him with their lips, but their hearts would be far from Him (Matthew 15:8). He also warned of those who serve two masters (Matthew 6:24). Psalm 144:11 warns of vain men who deceive with the "right hand of falsehood." In Psalm 12:2, David warned of those who speak with a "double heart." In James 1:8, James taught that "[a] double minded man is unstable in all his ways." In 1 Timothy 3:8, Paul referred to these same men as "double-tongued." For Leonard Sweet to exalt the "Father" of the New Age movement—Teilhard de Chardin—and suggest that Teilhard's way of seeing Christ is a "much more magnificent way" than our forefathers is to fall prey to our Adversary's deceptive devices. One thing is for sure: The New Age movement hasn't gone away—it has entered the church through men like Teilhard de Chardin and those like Sweet who exalt him as "Twentieth-century Christianity's major voice."

III. Leonard Sweet praises New Age leaders as his "role models" and "heroes."

While some Leonard Sweet defenders argue that his postmodern "New Light" apologetic flies right over the heads of "Old Light" "fundamentalist" types, the facts tell a different story. But what one learns in reading *Quantum Spirituality* is that Sweet wants to transform biblical Christianity into a quantum spirituality that is, in reality, a New Age/New Spirituality. Without any apology, Sweet writes that he is part of a "New Light" movement, and he describes those he especially admires as "New Light leaders." But many of Sweet's "New Light leaders" are New Age leaders who are in the process of overturning biblical Christianity through obliging New Age sympathizers like Leonard Sweet.

In the acknowledgments section of *Quantum Spirituality*, Leonard Sweet expresses his deep gratitude and admiration to various "New Light leaders" whom he openly praises as "the most creative religious leaders in America today." Included in this group are a number of men I was very familiar with from my years in the New Age—among them are Willis Harman, Matthew Fox, and M. Scott Peck. Sweet describes these three men—along with numerous other New Age figures cited—as "extraordinary" and "great" "New Light leaders." He goes so far as to say that they are his "personal role models" and "heroes" of "the true nature of the postmodern apologetic." Sweet writes:

> They are my personal role models (in an earlier day one
> could get away with "heroes") of the true nature of the

postmodern apologetic. More than anyone else, they have been my teachers on how to translate, without compromising content, the gospel into the indigenous context of the postmodern vernacular.[21]

But many of the men and women Leonard Sweet cited *have* compromised the "content" of the Gospel by translating it into the "postmodern vernacular" of a New Age/New Spirituality. For example, Willis Harman, Matthew Fox, and M. Scott Peck have all played leading roles in the initial establishment and popularization of the New Age/New Spirituality movement. But rather than *commending* these New Age/New Light leaders, a self-professing Christian leader like Sweet should be *warning* the church about them. A brief look at these three "New Light leaders" and their teachings will make this very clear.

Willis Harman (1918-1997)

Willis Harman is listed as one of the most influential Aquarian/New Age conspirators in Marilyn Ferguson's *The Aquarian Conspiracy.* Harman was a social scientist/futurist with the Stanford Research Institute and one of the chief architects of New Age thinking. He wrote the book *Global Mind Change: The New Age Revolution in the Way We Think.* A review by *The San Francisco Chronicle* on the front cover of the book reads: "There never has been a more lucid interpretation of New Age consciousness and what it promises for the future than the works of Willis Harman."[22]

Matthew Fox (1940-)

Another one of Sweet's self-described "role models" and "heroes" is Matthew Fox, a former Catholic priest who was dismissed from the Catholic church for openly professing heretical New Age teachings—teachings that include those of his revered mentor, Pierre Teilhard de Chardin. Fox, like Teilhard, teaches that all of creation is the "Cosmic Christ"—therefore the Cosmic Christ is "in" everyone and everything. In his book *The Coming of the Cosmic Christ*, Fox writes: "Divinity is found in all creatures"[23] and "We are all royal persons, creative, godly, divine, persons of beauty and of grace. We are all Cosmic Christs, 'other Christs.' But what good is this if we don't know it."[24] Leonard Sweet actually credits Fox in a footnote in *Quantum Spirituality* for inspiring Sweet's own description of the "cosmic body of Christ" and actually refers readers of *Quantum Spirituality* to Fox's New Age book *The Coming of the Cosmic Christ*.[25]

M. Scott Peck (1936-2005)

M. Scott Peck, the late psychiatrist and best-selling author of *The Road Less Traveled*, is another one of the "role models" and "heroes" that Leonard Sweet cites in his book *Quantum Spirituality*. *The Road Less Traveled* was on the *New York Times* best-seller list for over ten years. In a subsection of his book titled "The Evolution of Consciousness," Peck describes God as being "intimately associated with us—so intimately that He is part of us."[26] He also writes:

> If you want to know the closest place to look for grace, it is within yourself. If you desire wisdom greater than your own, you can find it inside you. . . . To put it plainly, our unconscious is God. God within us. We were part of God all the time.[27]

When Matthew Fox's *The Coming of the Cosmic Christ* was published in 1988, the lead endorsement on the back of Fox's book was written by M. Scott Peck. Peck and Fox were obviously in New Age agreement. Peck, like Fox and Sweet, describes Pierre Teilhard de Chardin in glowing terms. He describes Teilhard as "[p]erhaps the greatest prophet" of the "mystical," evolutionary leap that will take mankind toward "global consciousness" and "world community."[28] And it is this mystical New Age Christ of Pierre Teilhard de Chardin, Willis Harman, Matthew Fox, M. Scott Peck, and Leonard Sweet that challenges biblical Christianity today.

IV. Leonard Sweet thanks New Age Leader David Spangler for helping him develop his quantum spirituality's "new cell understanding of new light leadership."

> If we want to possess a magic crystal for our New Age work, we need look no further than our own bodies and the cells that make them up.[29] (David Spangler, 1991)

> I am grateful to David Spangler for his help in formulating this "new cell" understanding of New Light leadership.[30] (Leonard Sweet, 1991)

In his "A Response to Recent Misunderstandings," Leonard Sweet states: "Because I quote someone does not mean I agree with everything that person ever wrote." He goes on to say that "Some of the quotes I chose were meant to provide contrasting positions to my argument, some to buttress my argument, some even to mock my argument. The key consideration to whether I quoted someone was not 'Do I agree with them?' but 'Does this quote energize the conversation?' 'Guilt by association' is intellectually disreputable and injurious to the whole body of Christ." However, I would contend that there is a big difference between "guilt by *association*" and "guilt by *promotion*." Leonard Sweet is praising, thanking, and glorifying many of these New Age leaders—hardly guilt by association, especially when Sweet writes:

> I believe these are among the most creative religious leaders in America today. These are the ones carving out new channels for new ideas to flow. In a way this book was written to guide myself through their channels and chart their progress. The book's best ideas come from them.[31]

Ironically, one of the "channels" guiding him was an actual New Age channeler—David Spangler. A pioneering spokesperson for the New Age, Spangler has written numerous books over the years. His book *The Revelation: The Birth of the New Age* is a compilation of channeled transmissions that he received from his disembodied spirit guide "John." At one point in the book, Spangler documents what "John" prophesied about "the energies of the cosmic Christ" and Oneness:

> As the energies of the Cosmic Christ become increasingly manifest within the etheric life of Earth, many individuals will begin to respond with the realization that the Christ dwells within them. They will feel his presence moving within and through them and will begin to awaken to their heritage of Christhood and Oneness with God, the Beloved.[32]

In a postmodern-day consultation that bears more than a casual resemblance to King Saul's consult with the witch of Endor (1 Samuel 28), Leonard Sweet acknowledges in *Quantum Spirituality* that he was privately corresponding with New Age channeler David Spangler. Sweet even thanks Spangler for assisting him in forming his "new cell understanding" of "New Light leadership."[33] But as believers we are to "have no fellowship with the unfruitful works of darkness." Rather than thanking them, we are to reprove and expose them (Ephesians 5:11).

V. Misapplication of quantum physics tries to draw spiritual truth from physical theory.

Leonard Sweet—just like New Age leaders David Spangler and J. Z. Knight—tries to use quantum physics to prove that God indwells creation. He writes:

The coming together of the new biology and the new physics is providing the basic metaphors for this new global civilization that esteems and encourages whole-brain experiences, full-life expectations, personalized expressions, and a globalized consciousness.[34]

David Spangler writes:

When we experience such a quantum of transformation, we may simultaneously feel that the whole of the New Age is happening right now, that we are on the verge of overnight transformation—the fabled quantum leap into a new state of being.[35]

J.Z. Knight writes:

We have the epitome of a great science . . . quantum physics . . . Everyone is God.[36]

Tao of Physics

In his book *The Tao of Physics: An Explanation of the Parallels Between Modern Physics and Eastern Mysticism*, New Age physicist Fritjof Capra describes the union of mysticism and the new physics. He wrote "this kind of new spirituality is now being developed by many groups and movements, both within and outside the churches."[37] As an example of how this "new spirituality" is moving into the church, he actually cites one of Leonard Sweet's "role models" and "heroes"—Matthew Fox.[38]

When Sweet refers to the new biology and the new physics as "metaphors," he stretches these metaphors to the place of being actual fact. From his understanding of quantum physics, he asserts that all things are composed of energy and that this quantum energy must be God, hence God is embodied in all things. Yet, this metaphor falls on its face when we learn from Paul's writings that God and creation are two separate things as is illustrated in chapter one of Romans: "Who changed the truth of God into a lie, and worshipped and served the creature more than the Creator" (Romans 1:25).

Leonard Sweet and Rick Warren's "New Spirituality"

In their 1995 joint presentation *Tides of Change: Riding the Next Wave in Ministry,* Leonard Sweet and Rick Warren had a quantum conversation as they discussed "waves," "quantum metaphors," "revival," and what they were calling—even back then—a "New Spirituality." Sweet told Warren:

> Yeah, this is a wave period. I really love that metaphor of the wave and the wavelength. First of all, it is a quantum metaphor. It brings us out of the Newtonian world into this new science.[39]

Quantum waves, quantum wavelengths, quantum metaphors—all leading to a universal Quantum "God" and the Quantum New Age "Christ" of a New Gospel, New Spirituality, New Worldview, and ultimately a New World Religion that will be based on New Age teachings that seem to be scientific but are, in reality, "science falsely so called" (1 Timothy 6:20).

Conclusion

Teilhard de Chardin, Leonard Sweet, and an ever-growing band of New Age sympathizers would have us believe that all those who preceded us in the faith were unable to see the big picture, because, after all, they didn't have access to all the new scientific discoveries that we have today—scientific information that would have helped them gain the new spiritual understandings that Leonard Sweet claims to have acquired.

In that vein, Leonard Sweet, Rick Warren, and other church leaders are now teaching that God is in the process of bringing a "New Reformation"[40] and a "great spiritual awakening" and "revival" to the church. Sweet writes: "God is birthing the greatest spiritual awakening in the history of the church."[41] Yet this New Reformation and great awakening Sweet heralds, is falsely founded on his hybridized New Age Christianity with its "radical doctrine of embodiment of God in the very substance of creation."[42]

Ironically, while Sweet—as previously mentioned—encourages "a daily ritual" of standing in front of a mirror affirming "God is God and I am not," he at the same time tells people that, as a part of creation, God is embodied in them. He also encourages people to be "nudgers." He says "nudgers are not smudgers of the divine in people."[43] Nudgers help people discover their "inner Jesus."[44]

When the true Christ was asked what would be the sign of His coming and the end of the world, He said:

Take heed that no man deceive you. (Matthew 24:4)

He also said that many false prophets would arise and deceive many (Matthew 24:11). He specifically warned us to beware of false prophets who come in sheep's clothing. He said we would know them by their fruits.

Beware of false prophets, which come to you in sheep's clothing, but inwardly they are ravening wolves. Ye shall know them by their fruits. Do men gather grapes of thorns, or figs of thistles? (Matthew 7:15-16)

We must exhort one another daily. We must continue to preach the Word and not fall prey to those who would diminish the Word with their worldly wisdom, clever stories, metaphors, and false teachings.

Ye hypocrites, well did Esaias prophesy of you, saying, This people draweth nigh unto me with their mouth, and honoureth me with their lips; but their heart is far from me. But in vain they do worship me, teaching for doctrines the commandments of men. (Matthew 15: 7-9)

Every word of God is pure: he is a shield
unto them that put their trust in him. Add
thou not unto his words, lest he reprove thee,
and thou be found a liar. (Proverbs 30:5-6)

Eugene Peterson's Mixed Message

<hr>

Subversive Bible for a New Age

Eugene Peterson placed great emphasis on being—in his own words—"subversive." In a 1987 interview with *Christianity Today*, Peterson stated:

> So what I have tried to develop first of all, in myself, is the mentality of the subversive.[1]

"The Subversive Pastor" is the title of a chapter in his book *The Contemplative Pastor* (1989). *Subversive Spirituality* is the title of a book he released in 1994 while he was writing *The Message*. And if anyone doubts Peterson being a bit subversive, one need only look at his enthusiastic endorsements of three books with serious New Age implications—William Paul Young's *The Shack*, Rob Bell's universalistic *Love Wins*, and Sue Monk Kidd's *When the Heart Waits*. But many people would say—"So what? His *Message* translation has won the praise of everyone from Bono to Beth Moore to Billy Graham." But while Peterson delights many believers with what has been described as his "exegetical deftness," he has also introduced a lot of leaven—some of it decidedly New Age. And it is Peterson himself who warns—"And please don't toss this off as insignificant. It only takes a minute amount of yeast, you know, to permeate an entire loaf of bread" (Galatians 5:9 *MSG*). It is because of his leaven—particularly New Age leaven—that Peterson's *Message* is a spiritually dangerous *mixed Message*.

New Age References

As a former member of the New Age movement, I realize how easy it is for most believers to miss references to a belief system of which they were never a part and don't really understand. However, it is crucial we recognize *any* leaven—especially New Age leaven—when it appears in more recent Bible translations like *The Message* (1993, 2003), *The Voice* (2012), and *The Passion* (2017). A clear example of how New Age references and teachings are often hidden in plain sight is seen in *The Voice* translation of 2 Peter 3:18 when compared to, for example, the *King James Version*:

2 Peter 3:18

KJV

But grow in grace, and in the knowledge of our Lord and Saviour Jesus Christ. To him be glory both now and for ever.

The Voice

Instead, grow in grace and in the true knowledge of our Lord and Savior Jesus, the Anointed, to whom be glory, now and until the coming of the *new age*. (emphasis added)

King James

Eugene Peterson's *Message* was published by NavPress—the publishing arm of the longstanding Navigators organization. This Christian outreach was founded by the late evangelist Dawson Trotman (1906-1956). Highly respected, Trotman favored the *King James Version* in his teaching and preaching of God's Word.[2] In 2011, NavPress published *The Book of Proverbs: KJV/The Message*. The book presented comparative verses from *The Message* and the *King James Version* as it celebrated the *KJV* "as a cornerstone of the church, Western culture, and the development of the English language."[3] Given all this, and because of my own use of the *KJV*, this version will be used for the purposes of this chapter.

Examining Ten Variant Verses

I. As Above, So Below

Matthew 6:9-10

KJV

Our Father which art in heaven, Hallowed be thy name. Thy kingdom come. Thy will be done in earth, as it is in heaven.

MSG

Our Father in heaven, Reveal who you are. Set the world right; Do what's best—as above, so below.

What most people don't realize when reading this particular verse from *The Message* is that Eugene Peterson has inserted a several-thousand-year-old occult/New Age maxim into the mouth of Jesus Christ and into the Lord's Prayer. Instead of "in earth, as it is in heaven," Peterson translated it "as above, so below." This may seem harmless to most people, but as a former New Ager, I recognized "as above, so below" for what it was—an ancient mystical New Age concept that is said to be the key to all magic and all mysteries. It means that all is "One" because God is "in" everyone and everything. As already noted, this Doctrine of Oneness is the foundational teaching of the New Age/New World Religion. But universal Oneness is a New Age lie. God is not "*in*" everyone and everything. *As Above, So Below*—a book authored by the editors of the *New Age Journal* and published in 1992—summarizes the New Age significance of "as above, so below":

> Thousands of years ago in ancient Egypt, the great master alchemist Hermes Trismegistus, believed to be a contemporary of the Hebrew prophet Abraham, proclaimed this fundamental truth about the universe: "As above, so below; as below, so above." This maxim implies that the transcendent God beyond the physical universe and the immanent God within ourselves are one.[4]

When I initially searched the term "as above, so below" on the Internet, the first site that appeared said:

> This phrase comes from the beginning of The Emerald Tablet and embraces the entire system of traditional and modern magic which was inscribed upon the tablet in cryptic wording by Hermes Trismegistus. The significance of this phrase is that it is believed to hold the key to all mysteries. All systems of magic are claimed to function by this formula. "'That which is above is the same as that which is below' . . . The universe is the same as God, God is the same as man."[5]

Peterson Was Told

Because of all this, the question arises—Did anyone ever confront Peterson about using this New Age expression that, in effect, turns the Lord's Prayer into an occult/New Age prayer? The answer is yes. Soon after *The Message* was first published in 1993, a concerned reader wrote Peterson and asked him if he was aware that "as above, so below" was an occult/New Age term. Because my book *Deceived on Purpose* (2004) discussed this issue, the reader had contacted me and informed me that Peterson had written him back and said if he had known that "as above, so below" was a New Age term, he never would have used it. Certainly, Peterson—if he had truly cared—could have had it removed from subsequent printings of *The Message*. Yet, even now, three decades after his book first came out, "as above, so below," still remains in his translation—as do Peterson's references to Oneness and God being "in" everything.

II. Oneness: God "in" Everything

Ephesians 4:4-6

KJV

There is one body, and one Spirit, even as ye are called in one hope of your calling; One Lord, one faith, one baptism, One God and Father of all, who is above all, and through all, and in you all.

MSG

You were all called to travel on the same road and in the same direction, so stay together, both outwardly and inwardly. You have one Master, one faith, one baptism, one God and Father of all, who rules over all, works through all, and is present in all. Everything you are and think and do is permeated with Oneness.

New Age Doctrine of Oneness

By not removing "as above, so below" from *The Message*, Peterson actually reinforces its New Age meaning by translating Ephesians 4:4-6 to state that God is universally "present in all" and that "Everything you are and think and do is permeated with Oneness." The "God" of the New Age, channeled through one of his top leaders, describes those who introduce the concept of Oneness (God "in" everything) as the "messengers," "visionaries," and "heralds of a New Age."[6]

In the *KJV*, Ephesians 4:6 states "in *you* all" to make it clear that Paul is only speaking to "the saints which are at Ephesus, and to the faithful in Christ Jesus" (Ephesians 1:1). He is not stating that God is universally present in everyone and that a universal Oneness pervades everything we "are and think and do." Rather, he is specifically talking to believers to whom the Holy Spirit had been previously sent because of their commitment to Jesus Christ (John 15:26). Paul is not making a statement about Oneness and God being "present in all." In a published interview, Peterson said that one of the breakthrough moments in his knowing that he could create a new translation of the Bible was when he realized how "easy" it would be for him to "untangle" the apostle Paul:

> Maybe I could do Paul, because Paul is easy in a sense because he gets tangled up and you can untangle him.[7]

The irony is that in trying to "untangle" Paul in Ephesians 4:4-6 (as if Paul needed untangling), Peterson is the one who gets all tangled up as he ends up presenting a mixed New Age message instead of the gospel truth. In another *Message* verse with special New Age implications, Peterson's Jesus is never described as Lord.

III. The "Master Jesus"

John 13:13

KJV

Ye call me Master and Lord: and ye say well; for so I am.

MSG

You address me as "Teacher" and "Master," and rightly so.
That is what I am.

The late New Age leader, Benjamin Creme, taught that Jesus is not the Christ but rather a "disciple" of Christ. Creme explained that when the New Age Christ appears, he will not come as "Savior," but as "Teacher," and in his own name—which is exactly what the true Christ said would happen (John 5:43). New Age leaders like Creme teach that this New Age Christ will *set things right* by teaching everyone the Doctrine of Oneness—that God is immanent "in man and all creation"—and that he is present in all religions. Creme wrote:

> But eventually a new world religion will be inaugurated which will be a fusion and synthesis of the approach of the East and the approach of the West. The Christ will bring together, not simply Christianity and Buddhism, but the concept of God transcendent—outside of His creation—and also the concept of God immanent in all creation—in man and all creation.[8]

In explaining how Jesus was not the Christ but rather his disciple, Creme described how the first century Jesus allowed the "Christ" to "overshadow" him and work through him after he was baptized by John. Counterfeiting the true Christ's return with his "mighty angels" (2 Thessalonians 1:7), Creme explained that when the New Age Christ appears he will come with his "twelve Masters of Wisdom." These Masters—one of whom will be the "Master Jesus"—will help the New Age Christ do his work in the world. Thus, according to Creme and other New Age leaders, "Jesus" is not the "Lord" and he is not the "Christ"—he is simply the "Master Jesus."

Creme—speaking for this New Age Christ—explains how this "Master Jesus" will assume the throne of St. Peter and head up the "Christian" Church which will be centered in Rome as part of the New World Religion. Creme stated that the "Master Jesus"—obviously a false Jesus—will be in charge of a New Reformation. It will be his job to "reform the Christian churches"[9] so they conform to the "new reality" of the New World Religion which the return of the false Christ and his Masters will create.[10]

New Age leaders have made it clear that in the New Age/New Spirituality/New World Religion, you can identify yourself with any or no religion as long as you confess that "we are all One" because "God is in everyone and everything." And, of course, you must profess that the New Age Christ—not Jesus Christ—is your Lord.

In light of all this, it is important to note that *The Message* never refers to Jesus *as* Lord—not even once. Consistent with New Age teachings, Peterson's Jesus is repeatedly referred to as the "Master Jesus." And while the disciples of the true Jesus Christ called him Master, it was always with the understanding that He was also their Lord—and they continually and constantly addressed Him as such. And even when they addressed Him as Master, they never referred to Him as the "Master Jesus." Yet the term "Master Jesus" appears repeatedly in passage after passage in *The Message*. An example of this is in Revelation 22:20-21:

KJV

Even so, come, Lord Jesus. The grace of our Lord Jesus Christ be with you all. Amen.

MSG

Yes! Come, Master Jesus! The grace of the Master Jesus be with all of you. Oh, Yes!

When "as above, so below," "Oneness," "God in everything," "Master Jesus," and all the other occult elements of the New Age/New Spirituality are taken as a whole, occultists collectively describe it as the "Great Work"—another mixed message found in *The Message.*

IV. Great Work

Philippians 1:6

KJV

Being confident of this very thing, that he which hath begun a good work in you will perform it until the day of Jesus Christ.

MSG

There has never been the slightest doubt in my mind that the God who started this great work in you would keep at it and bring it to a flourishing finish on the very day Christ Jesus appears.

"Great Work" in *The Message*

The Greek word *agathos* in Philippians 1:6 is commonly translated into English as "good"—not "great." But in this passage, Peterson translates agathos as "great"—not "good." Thus, it becomes a "great work" that God is doing in you—not "good work." Yet when he translated this same word agathos twenty-one verses previous in Ephesians 6:8, he translated it "good"—rather than "great." Of the more than fifty Gateway Bible versions listed on the Internet, all but three translated Philippians 1:6 as "good work." The three that translated it "great work" were the more recent controversial translations—*The Voice*, *The Passion*, and *The Message*.

"Great Work" in the New Age

The term "great work" that Eugene Peterson inserted into Philippians 1:6 is yet another New Age term like "as above, so below" that is hidden in plain sight. Terms like "as above, so below," "Oneness," and "great work" might seem inconsequential to most Christians—but they are not. They are a part of the emerging and overlapping language of the New Age/New Gospel/New World Religion reminiscent of the one language that God found so reprehensible in Babel:

> And the LORD said, Behold, the people is one, and they have all one language; and this they begin to do: and now nothing will be restrained from them, which they have imagined to do. (Genesis 11:6)

The first entry that arose when I searched the Internet for "Great Work" immediately connected it with the "as above, so below" teachings of Hermeticism and the New Age/New Spirituality.[11] In *False Christ Coming: Does Anybody Care?* (2011), I quote the false Christ Maitreya inviting everyone to "share" in his "Great Work" of transforming the world. He said:

> Share with Me, My friends, in a Great Work—nothing less than the transformation of this world.[12]

Also in *False Christ Coming*, I described how New Age leader (and 2020 Democratic presidential primary candidate) Marianne Williamson invokes this same occult/New Age term "Great

Work" in her 2000 book *Healing the Soul of America*. She describes how the evolution of humanity will come through the enactment of the esoteric traditions collectively referred to as the "Great Work":

> Beyond the appearances of history, there is a great and glorious unfolding plan for the destiny of nations. According to the mystical traditions, God carries this plan within His mind, seeking always, in every way, channels for its furtherance. His plan for the evolution of humanity, and the preparation of teachers to guide it, is called within the esoteric traditions the Great Work.[13]

Another New Age source describes how the completion of the "Great Work" will be accomplished when it has been introduced in multiple ways "across numerous fields":

> The so-called "Great Work" of the occultists is at the heart of all esoteric activities in both the East and the West. And the "completion" of this "Great Work" is alluded to via a multiplicity of euphemisms scattered across numerous fields.[14]

"Great Work" in Gospel Music

The term "Great Work" has been introduced not only into three contemporary Bible translations, but also into contemporary Christian music. The album and title song "A Great Work" were both nominated for 2018 Dove and 2019 Grammy awards as the song for "best contemporary gospel song" and the album for "best contemporary gospel album." Featuring Philippians 1:6 as the centerpiece of his album and song, popular Christian recording artist Brian Courtney Wilson sings: "He that has begun a great work in you is faithful to perform it." In what has been described as his "purpose-driven lyrics,"[15] the term "great work" is repeated over fifty times by the singer and the accompanying choir.[16] This popular hit song is another graphic example of how an overlapping New Age term has become part of our day-to-day "Christian" language. But this is the way Satan, the Devil, Lucifer—also known as the "light-bearer"—works.

V. Light-bearer

Matthew 5:15

KJV

Neither do men light a candle, and put it under a bushel, but on a candlestick; and it giveth light unto all that are in the house.

MSG

If I make you light-bearers, you don't think I'm going to hide you under a bucket do you? I'm putting you on a light stand.

In my Internet search for the definition of light-bearer, I was immediately directed to the name Lucifer.[17] An online thesaurus listed the following synonyms for the word "light-bearer"—Lucifer, Beelzebub, Devil, Prince of Darkness, and Tempter.[18] The occult/New Age Theosophical Society published a monthly journal as far back as the late 1800s titled *Lucifer* that featured a front-cover banner that read—"The Light-bearer is the Morning Star or Lucifer."[19] The Canadian branch of this same Theosophical Society continues to publish their seasonal magazine titled *The Light Bearer*.[20] And the late New Age channeler Elizabeth Clare Prophet's Summit Lighthouse organization advertised their 2018 annual conference by proclaiming—"Lightbearers of the World Unite."[21] Even a "Lightbearer" coffee mug with what was described as a "unique esoteric satanic 666 Luciferian seal symbol" can be purchased online. The product description further reads:

> Lucifer the Lightbearer Satanic Mug—perfect gift for you or someone dear to you.[22]

Like light-bearer and the other terms already mentioned, "golden circle" is yet one more mixed message with occult/New Age implications found in *The Message.*

VI. Golden Circle

Revelation 2:5

KJV

Remember therefore from whence thou art fallen, and repent, and do the first works; or else I will come unto thee quickly, and will remove thy candlestick out of his place, except thou repent.

MSG

Do you have any idea how far you've fallen? A Lucifer fall! Turn back! Recover your dear early love. No time to waste, for I'm well on my way to removing your light from the golden circle.

The term "golden circle" is not found in the original manuscripts. In fact, the single word "circle" is found only once in the *KJV* and refers to the circumference of the earth (Isaiah 40:22). An Internet search for "golden circle" does not bring up anything that equates to being biblical. But it does connect the term to, among other things, a Masonic ritual, a secret society, and modern-day witchcraft. "The Order of the Golden Circle" is the women's auxiliary of the 33 degree Scottish Rite of Freemasonry.[23] The "Knights of the Golden Circle" was a radical secret society in mid-nineteenth century America,[24] and Wiccans—with their "golden chalk" and "golden energy"—often invoke the term "as above, so below" to seal their "ritual circles":

> When Witches seal a circle casting, sacred space or a spell, they often say the words *"As above, so below."*[25]

> The Maxim *"As above, so below"* (as well as others you'll study in the future) does tell us that Wicca carries with it into the twenty-first century a heavy coil of very old, very ancient, golden energy.[26]

> Golden chalk is used to draw the heart glyph at the center of a ritual circle. Golden chalk is crafted in a witches' cauldron.[27]

And just as Peterson added the term "golden circle" in translating Revelation 2:5, he added the word "green" to his translation of Romans 15:13.

VII. God of Green Hope

Romans 15:13

KJV

Now the God of hope fill you with all joy and peace in believing, that ye may abound in hope, through the power of the Holy Ghost.

MSG

Oh! May the God of green hope fill you up with joy, fill you up with peace, so that your believing lives, filled with the life-giving energy of the Holy Spirit, will brim over with hope!

Green New Age

The word "green" for most people has come to mean recycling, reducing our carbon footprint, and overall good stewardship of the earth. However, in recent times, the word "green" has also come to represent some of the more extreme environmental activism and earth worship identified with Paganism, Witchcraft, and the New Age movement. One online site straightforwardly states that the word "green" is synonymous with the term New Age:

> Not everyone who came to be associated with the New Age phenomenon openly embraced the term "New Age" . . . Other terms that were employed synonymously with "New Age" in this milieu included "Green."[28]

The "Green Movement" is commonly associated with Gaia and earth worship and has been described as being "at the very heart of the Global Green Agenda."[29] Consistent with New Age teachings, Gaia philosophy is the belief that humanity can save "Mother Earth" by recognizing its Oneness with "her." Gaia is acknowledged to be part of the "Green Agenda" for a united "Green Religion." The all-encompassing "Green Movement" is presently and actively promoting current environmental policies. Popular with progressive politicians and New Age spiritualists, a "Green New Deal" is already in the works. There is also a "Green Witchcraft,"[30] and the "Green Horned God" of Wicca is frequently referred to as the "Green Man."[31]

Peterson's "God of green hope" translation lends itself to all of the above as it conveniently meshes with Paganism, Witchcraft, and the New Age movement. The Bible warns that we cannot just add words like "as above, so below," "golden circle," and "green" that are not in the original manuscripts and call it a paraphrase or a translation (Proverbs 30:6). It is as wrong as describing God's creation as "God-craft."

VIII. God-Craft

Psalm 19:1

KJV

The heavens declare the glory of God; and the firmament sheweth his handiwork.

MSG

God's glory is on tour in the skies, God-craft on exhibit across the horizon.

Peterson's introduction of the term "God-craft" seems to offer a euphemistic olive branch to those practicing witchcraft. In two videos posted by a self-professing "Christian witch," he describes how he mixes his faith in "Christ" with his faith in witchcraft. He used the same overlapping term used by Peterson in *The Message* to describe his faith as "more of a God-craft":

> Many people don't necessarily understand how you can mix Christianity and the love of Christ with a word like magic, and power, or the craft or the label Christian witch.[32]

> Do I believe, do I practice a form of the craft? Yes I do, but I believe its more of a God-craft than it is, say, what most people would determine as witchcraft.[33]

Thus, Peterson's translation of the Psalm 19:1 verse that reads "God-craft on exhibit across the horizon" seems more suggestive of witches riding the night skies than the heavens declaring God's glory. Peterson has not only added terms like "as above, so below," "golden circle" and "God-craft," but he has also removed important phrases like "cunningly devised fables" and replaced them with misleading substitutes like "wishing on a star."

IX. Wishing on a Star

2 Peter 1:16

KJV

For we have not followed cunningly devised fables, when we made known unto you the power and coming of our Lord Jesus Christ, but were eyewitnesses of his majesty.

MSG

We weren't, you know, just wishing on a star when we laid the facts out before you regarding the powerful return of our Master, Jesus Christ. We were there for the preview! We saw it with our own eyes.

It doesn't take a Bible scholar to see that the key phrase "cunningly devised fables" was removed and the meaning of the passage completely changed by Eugene Peterson. "We weren't, you know, just wishing on a star" bears no resemblance to "For we have not followed cunningly devised fables." Peterson's "wishing on a star" sounds more like Walt Disney and Pinocchio than the apostle Peter. What was a strong biblical warning about spiritual deception now sounds more like an indirect reference to Jiminy Cricket.

Those of us who were formerly involved in the New Age movement were not "wishing on a star" regarding the "coming of Christ." We were following a "cunningly devised fable"—a "new story" and a "new narrative" for the coming New Age. This "cunningly devised" New Age/New Gospel fable convinced us that we were all "One" because God was "in" everyone and everything. But Peterson chose to eliminate this sharp as a two-edged sword warning about "cunningly devised fables," replacing it with the dull-as-a-butter knife reference to "wishing on a star."

The best-selling book *The Shack* is a perfect example of a cunningly devised fable. William Paul Young's "Jesus" presents the same deceptive "as above, so below" teaching found in *The Message*—that God is "in" everyone and everything. Young's "Jesus" says, "God, who is the ground of all being, dwells in, around, and through all things."[34] Not surprisingly, Eugene Peterson—the man who removed the apostle Peter's warning about "cunningly devised fables"—provides a glowing front cover endorsement for William Paul Young's cunningly devised fable!

Eugene Peterson, in using phrases like "as above, so below," "light-bearer," and "God-craft" has created confusion with terms that overlap with the occult and the New Age. It was Peterson, himself, who warned:

> We cannot be too careful about the words we use; we start out using them and then they end up using us.[35]

But if you question today's Christian leaders regarding any of this, you may find yourself being labeled as "defiant" and "mutinous."

X. Defiant or Mutinous

Proverbs 24:21-22

KJV

My son, fear thou the LORD and the king: and meddle not with them that are given to change: For their calamity shall rise suddenly; and who knoweth the ruin of them both?

MSG

Fear God, dear child—respect your leaders; don't be defiant or mutinous. Without warning your life can turn upside down, and who knows how or when it might happen?

One of the predominant ways the New Age has entered the church is through new translations like *The Message* that change the meaning of otherwise properly translated Scripture. Somehow, we are to just trust that these paraphrases or translations have only our best interest in mind. Proverbs 24:21-22 warns of the ruinous consequences for getting involved with change-agent leaders who are "given to change." Yet, Eugene Peterson removes the reference to change and, instead, warns of the ruinous consequences for not following these change-agent leaders! Those not respecting their leaders are described as "defiant" and "mutinous" and as a result may find their lives being turned "upside down." But the only way Peterson can come up with this translation is to turn the original Hebrew upside down.

It is not "mutinous" or "defiant" to search the Scriptures to see if what these leaders are saying is "so" (Acts 17:11). Isaiah specifically warned about leaders who were leading people astray:

> O my people, they which lead thee cause thee to err, and
> destroy the way of thy paths. (Isaiah 3:12)

He further warned that ruinous destruction would not come to those who defied these errant leaders but to those who unquestioningly followed them:

> For the leaders of this people cause them to err; and they
> that are led of them are destroyed. (Isaiah 9:16)

A Dangerous Walk

The danger of entrusting one's Christian walk to Eugene Peterson and his *Message* paraphrase/translation was dramatically underscored in a 2007 book Peterson wrote titled *The Jesus Way*. In describing a group hike he took with friends and family in Glacier National Park, Peterson discloses how he purposely withheld crucial information from his family and friends prior to their setting out on their walk. In a moment of almost inexplicable candor, Peterson reveals how he "relished the spurt of adrenaline" he experienced in not telling his fellow hikers how a grizzly bear had mauled a hiker just the week before on the very same trail they were about to take. What makes his account especially disturbing is that his group included a friend's two-year-old child and his pregnant daughter-in-law. Peterson wrote:

> A few years ago a grizzly attacked a hiker not far from our home and mauled him badly. The hiker had heard of the wonder and beauty of the mountains of Montana and drove across the country from North Carolina to experience them for himself. Interviewed from his hospital bed, he said, "I'm never coming back to this place!" He didn't know that wonder and beauty can also be dangerous.
>
> A week after that grizzly mauling, Jan and I along with our son and his wife, plus another friend with her two-year-old son, were hiking on that same trail. At the trailhead a notice was posted: "Danger: Grizzly activity on this trail. Hike at your own risk." None of the others knew of the previous week's mauling and I didn't say anything. I relished the spurt of adrenaline. The danger to life heightens the sense of life.[36]

Peterson goes on to describe how the group later encountered a grizzly bear and her cub that were up the trail from where they were walking. Obviously, concerned for her safety and that of her unborn child, Peterson's pregnant daughter-in-law insisted on leaving immediately. Peterson attempts to use the incident to illustrate how the beauty of one's surroundings can also be a threat to the "fragility and preciousness of life." He explains that "Holy ground" can also be "dangerous ground":

> And then Amy, our daughter-in-law, who was five months pregnant and therefore especially aware of the fragility and preciousness of life, said, "I want to get out of here." And we did get out. Holy ground, but dangerous ground.[37]

And while Peterson waxes poetic about the mix of beauty and danger inherent in life, his point falls flat as an obvious question arises—What kind of a man would put others in harm's way for his own personal adrenalin rush? As I read Peterson's strange account, I realized the incident was a perfect metaphor for what I had come to believe about Peterson and his *Message* translation. You are walking on a very dangerous path when you choose to walk with Eugene Peterson—whether it is in Glacier National Park or through the pages of his *Message* "Bible."

> For we are not as many, which corrupt the word of God: but as of sincerity, but as of God, in the sight of God speak we in Christ. (2 Corinthians 2:17)

For the time will come when they will not
endure sound doctrine; but after their own
lusts shall they heap to themselves teachers,
having itching ears; And they shall turn
away their ears from the truth, and shall
be turned unto fables. (2 Timothy 4:3-4)

Shack Theology– Universalism and Fractal Oneness

The Shack, written and published in 2007 by William Paul Young, has sold over twenty-two million copies and remains a best-seller today. Many Christians have purchased multiple copies and given them to friends and family.

The Shack reads as a true story but is obviously allegorical fiction. The book conveys postmodern spiritual ideas and teachings that challenge biblical Christianity—all in the name of "God" and "Jesus" and the "Holy Spirit." Author William Paul Young's alternative presentation of traditional Christianity has both inspired and outraged his many readers.

Much like New Age author James Redfield's book *The Celestine Prophecy*, *The Shack* is a fictional vehicle for upending certain biblical concepts and presenting contrary unbiblical scenarios. Allegorical novels can be a clever way to present truth. They can also be used to present things that are not true. Some books like *The Shack* do both.

I was drawn into the New Age movement years ago by books and lectures containing parabolic stories that were not unlike *The Shack*. They felt spiritually uplifting as they tackled tough issues and talked about God's love and forgiveness. They seemed to provide me with what I spiritually needed as they gave me much needed hope and promise. Building on the credibility they achieved through their inspirational and emotive writings, my New Age authors and teachers would then go on to tell me that God is "in" everyone and everything.

I discovered that author William Paul Young does exactly the same thing in *The Shack*. He moves through his very engaging and emotional story to eventually present this same New Age teaching. He writes:

> God who is the ground of all being, dwells in, around, and through all things.[1]

When People Say *The Shack* Is Just a Novel

I went to see *The Shack* movie when it was made into a film in 2017. A woman standing in line outside the theater was eager to talk with me about William Paul Young's best-selling book. She said she "loved" *The Shack* and couldn't understand why it had so many critics on the Internet. She was especially perplexed by the number of negative comments made by pastors. Obviously confused by all the controversy, she suddenly exclaimed—"But *The Shack* is just a novel!"

What the woman and so many other *Shack* readers fail to consider is that the book is much more than "just a novel." It is a carefully crafted presentation of William Paul Young's alternative "Christian" universalist theology based on "real" conversations he claims to have had with God. In Young's foreword to *The Shack Revisited*, a book written by his friend C. Baxter Kruger, Young corrects any misunderstanding that *The Shack* is just a novel. He writes:

> Please don't misunderstand me; *The Shack* is theology.
> But it is theology wrapped in story.[2]

If you want to understand better the perspectives and theology that frame *The Shack,* this book [Kruger's] is for you. Baxter has taken on the incredible task of exploring the nature and character of the God who met me in my own shack.[3]

According to Young, God came to him in the "Great Sadness" of his own personal "shack" and communicated directly with him. Much of *The Shack*'s theology is based on what Young learned in his conversations with "God."

William Paul Young's Conversations With "God"

A Christian news source reprinted excerpts from several posts Young made on his personal blog back in August 2007. In these excerpts, Young explained that *The Shack* is a story, but it is a story based on real conversations he was having with God, his friends, and his family. He writes:

> Remember, I am thinking about writing this for my kids, so I am searching for a good vehicle to communicate through. I figure a good story would be great . . . but I didn't have one. So I started with what I did have . . . conversations. So, off and on, for about three months I wrote down conversations; *conversations that I was having with God* mostly, but which often included friends or family.[4] (emphasis added)

> Is the story "real"? The story is fiction. I made it up. Now, having said that, I will add that the emotional pain with all its intensity and the process that tears into Mack's heart and soul are very real. I have my "shack," the place I had to go through to find healing. I have my Great Sadness . . . that is all real. *And the conversations are very real and true. . . .*

So is the story true? The pain, the loss, the grief, the process, the conversations, the questions, the anger, the longing, the secrets, the lies, the forgiveness . . . all real, all true.[5] (emphasis added)

Young's "Christian" Universalism

In a February 16, 2008 post on a blog called *Christian Universalism: The Beautiful Heresy,* an avowed "friend" corroborates Young's 2007 blog post about his conversations with God. The friend describes how the conversations Young's main character Mack has with God in *The Shack* are "real conversations" that Young actually had with God. She reveals how these conversations "revolutionized" Young, his family, and friends such as herself. She says that the "radically dangerous" teachings that Young put in his novel have become her new "systematic theology" and *The Shack* is her new "systematic theology handbook." The following are her exact words and punctuation as they were originally posted on the *Christian Universalism* blog:

> I know the author well—a personal friend. (Our whole house church devoured it [*The Shack*] last summer, and Paul came to our home to discuss it—WONDERFUL time!) The conversations that "Mack" has with God, are real conversations that Paul Young had with God . . . and they revolutionized him, his family, and friends (Paul had a very traumatic past, raised by missionary parents, who left him in the care of the stone-age Dani tribe, while they did "God's work." He was abused by them, in the process—and there were other tragedies in his life, later on. When he was a broken mess, God began to speak to him). He wrote the story (rather than a "sermon") to give the real conversations context—and because Jesus also used simple stories to engage our hearts, even by-passing our objective brains,

in order to have His message take root in our hearts, and grow. . . .

I had already come to believe all the "radically dangerous" teachings within this book—so it mostly confirmed what I already believed. But, it most definitely highlighted the reality that I don't yet KNOW (KNOW!) how much God loves me. I want the relationship with God that I see in Paul Young's life. . . . This was the first book that I read straight through 4 times. First to absorb it. Secondly, to underline. Third to highlight. Fourth, to put "headers" on the top of each page, so that I could find certain passages again. It's become my new "systematic theology" handbook.[6]

Thus, by his own account and that of his friend, William Paul Young would be the first to deny that *The Shack* is "just a novel."

Young the Universalist

Back to my conversation with the woman in front of the movie theater. When she said that *The Shack* was "just a novel," I described how his novel was actually a fictional device used as a "vehicle" for presenting some of his own misguided theological teachings—teachings that had more in common with New Age teachings than biblical Christianity. When she acknowledged knowing about the New Age movement, I told her that some of *The Shack's* teachings were actually New Age teachings. But before I could explain what those specific teachings were and how I had once been involved in the New Age myself, the theater doors opened, the line started moving, and our conversation was suddenly over. She seemed relieved as she turned toward the theater and away from me.

Praying that she would come to understand that William Paul Young has more in common with New Age universalism than biblical Christianity, I had no idea at the time that Young was about to publicly declare in a new book what so many of us already knew. In *Lies We Believe About God*, which was released on March 7th, 2017 Young states that he believes in "universal salvation"[7] and that "every single human being is in Christ" and "Christ is in them."[8] Thus, Young himself makes it very clear that *The Shack* is not "just a novel" but rather a cunningly devised fable (2 Peter 1:16) for presenting some of his own heretical universalistic New Age views.

Young's Universal New Age Lie–Christ "In" Everyone

Young Publicly Endorses Universal Salvation

In his book *Lies We Believe About God*, William Paul Young openly describes himself as a universalist. In chapter 13, Young would have us believe it is a "lie" to tell someone, "You need to get saved."[9] Young asks himself the rhetorical questions, "Are you suggesting that everyone is saved? That you believe in universal salvation?"[10] He answers, "That is exactly what I am saying!"[11] Young then goes on to teach that "every single human being is in Christ" and that "Christ is in them."[12] With this unbiblical teaching, one recalls how Young put these same heretical "God in everything" words in the mouth of his "Jesus" character in *The Shack* when he wrote:

> God, who is the ground of all being, dwells in, around, and through all things.[13]

The Trinitarian Lie

Young would have us believe his trinitarian lie that God, Jesus, and the Holy Spirit inherently indwell everyone.[14] This is exactly what the false "Christ" of the New Age teaches. In fact, it is the foundational teaching of the New Age/New Spirituality/New World Religion that has progressively moved into the world and into the church. And as we saw, TBN was only too glad to bring William Paul Young's *Shack* theology to their countless viewers.

Shack, TBN, and the New Age Lie

In 2017, Trinity Broadcasting Network provided William Paul Young with the world's largest "Christian" stage—his very own television series on TBN. Young's *Restoring The Shack* episodes were masterfully produced on location in beautiful Montana. His presentations were underscored and enhanced with soothing music that was clearly designed to evoke a strong emotional response and positive assent from viewers to whatever Young was preaching or teaching.

In what could also be described as "The Shack Show," Young brought his own weekly brand of *Shack* promotion, *Shack* theology, and *Shack* therapy to TBN viewers as he hoped to convert them from their own "Great Sadness" to his own relational take on what used to be biblical Christianity. The real sadness is that Young's *Shack* theology and *Shack* therapy have more to do with his love for universalism and New Agey trinitarianism than it does with scriptural truth. Why New Agey? Because when Young teaches about "relationship" he is, by his own *Shack* definition, referring to the Trinity within—a God and Christ and Holy Spirit that are said to be "in" everyone and everything.[15]

Somewhat elusive about exposing his own personal Universalism in the past, Young made himself very clear on the matter in his book, *Lies We Believe About God*. Nevertheless, TBN was only too pleased to not only promote this book, but to also use it as a fundraiser for themselves at the same time.

Shack Therapy: William Paul Young, Kahlil Gibran, and "The Great Sadness"

William Paul Young writes that *The Shack* is "theology wrapped in story."[16] And his *Shack* theology presents a universalistic *Shack Therapy* for the "Great Sadness" that plagues his main character "Mack." Young remarks in numerous interviews that, like Mack, most people have their own inner "shack" where they store their secrets and their own personal "Great Sadness." This "Great Sadness" becomes Young's personal metaphor for the inner pain and anguish locked within his and other people's souls. Lebanese-American writer, artist, philosopher, and universalist Kahlil Gibran (1883-1931) used this same phrase—"great sadness"—in his 1926 book *The Madman: His Parables and Poems*. He wrote:

> Then a great sadness came over the face of my soul, and into her voice.[17]

In the Acknowledgments section of *The Shack*, Young thanks Kahlil Gibran for his "creative stimulation." He quotes Gibran not only in *The Shack*, but also in opening the very first chapter of his second novel *Crossroads*. Kahlil Gibran is best known for his perennial best-seller, *The Prophet*—a book that "has long been one of the bibles of the New-Age movement."[18] As a matter of fact, as former New Agers, Gibran's book was a treasured part of our New Age library. What's more, "New Age Pioneer" was the title of a 1998 *New York Times* book review about Gibran and his New Age influence.[19] Robin Waterfield, an authority on Gibran and a consulting editor for religious and New Age publishers, wrote a definitive biography on Gibran that was the subject of the aforementioned *New York Times* book review. Waterfield's book, *Prophet: The Life and Times of Kahlil Gibran*, described the biographer's belief that Gibran was highly influential in the initial formation of the New Age movement:

> I suggest that Gibran has been one of the hidden influences on the New Age . . . I cannot say that without him the New Age movement would not have arisen, but it is, I think, safe to say that he has had an enormous influence on it.[20]

> I think it is arguable that Gibran was one of the founding fathers of the New Age.[21]

Young Wants to Be More Like Oprah?

Ten years after the release of *The Shack*, William Paul Young declared he was a believer in universal salvation.[22] Sounding much like any New Age universalist, Young is teaching the panentheistic and heretical New Age doctrines of Christ "in" everyone[23] and God "in" all things.[24] With *The Shack* being made into a movie and with *Shack* book sales now over 22 million copies, with countless radio and television interviews, church talks, and with his own *Restoring The Shack* TBN prime time television series under his belt, Young had done just about everything except appear on *Oprah*. But then he also did that.

On July 9, 2017, Young was the featured guest on Oprah Winfrey's *Super Soul Sunday* television program.[25] The day after the program, Young suddenly announced—"I want to be more like Oprah."[26] And with that statement *Shack* lovers should be shocked that an avowed "Christian" would want to be "more like Oprah"—one of the most influential New Age leaders in the world today.[27] But what most people don't realize is that in regard to New Age universalism, William Paul Young is *already* like Oprah—and Kahlil Gibran—and this may be one of the greatest "Great Sadnesses" of all.

A Cat Named Judas

The name *Judas* has been described as the most hated name in all the world. Except for *Shack* author William Paul Young and maybe a few exceptional others, hardly anybody ever names anyone or anything Judas. It is one of those forbidden names like Jezebel or Lucifer that most people would never dream of naming their child, their dog—or their cat. The very name denotes a sense of treachery and betrayal. After all, Judas was the one who openly betrayed Jesus and paved the way for His crucifixion. So what was Young thinking? Why does *The Shack*'s most endearing character—Missy—have a cat named Judas?[28] And it seems especially odd to have a cat with that name in a family where the mother's faith is described as "deep"[29] and Missy is asking sincere questions about Jesus' death.[30]

Heresy and Betrayal

As cited, Young contends that *The Shack* is much more than a novel; he describes *The Shack* as "theology wrapped in story." He writes:

> Please don't misunderstand me; *The Shack* is theology. But it is theology wrapped in story, the Word becoming flesh and living inside the blood and bones of common human experience.[31]

This is said in spite of the fact that Young's *Shack* characters and universalistic *Shack* "theology" frequently mock God and God's Word with their cryptic humor and clever interplay. To be perfectly blunt, the name Judas fits right in with much of what Young is teaching. Like Judas, Young betrays Jesus Christ and biblical Christianity with his heretical *Shack* theology—where there is, among other things, no Devil and no Christ. Neither of these words can be found anywhere in the whole *Shack* story. The Devil is never mentioned because Young would have us believe that evil and darkness "do not have any actual existence."[32] And *The Shack's* "Jesus" is never identified as Christ. In fact, the name of Christ is nowhere to be found in the whole *Shack* story.

One well-known pastor gave an impassioned sermon about thirteen heresies he found in *The Shack*.[33] One heresy he did not mention is perhaps the most egregious of all—the panentheistic proposition that God is "in" all things. Incredibly, Young puts this foundational doctrine of the New Age/New Spirituality/New World Religion right in the mouth of *The Shack's* "Jesus." Young's "Jesus" states—"God, who is the ground of all being, dwells in, around, and through all things."[34] But this is a false teaching. God is not "in" all things. For Young to put these heretical words in the mouth of *The Shack's* "Jesus" is an absolute betrayal of the true Jesus Christ.

Thus, as William Paul Young plays fast and loose with biblical Christianity, should we be surprised that he plays fast and loose with a name like Judas—a name that perfectly describes Young's role in today's wayward church. What Young describes as "theology wrapped in story" is really biblical betrayal wrapped in a cunningly devised fable (2 Peter 1:16). *The Shack* is everything that the true Jesus Christ warned us to watch out for when he said to "be not deceived" (Luke 21:8). And that warning would seem to include authors like William Paul Young who think nothing at all about putting heretical New Age doctrines in Jesus' mouth and naming a little girl's cat Judas.

Fractals, Chaos Theory, Quantum Spirituality, & *The Shack*

A number of years ago, after speaking at a church service, a young woman approached me and told me she had discovered something interesting in *The Shack* and had written a short article about it. She asked if I would be willing to read her article. I told her I would.

Back home a week later, I found her paper in my notebook. I was intrigued by the title—"Fractal Theory in The Shack." In her article, she explains that during her research she had rented a DVD movie, which she had been told had New Age undertones. She then describes something she discovered in the movie:

> In the movie *The Seeker* a young boy is a chosen one who is to find signs hidden throughout time, which will help fight against the encroaching darkness. . . . [I]n the movie, each sign that the boy is to find is known as a fractal. When I heard the term fractal, right away I realized that I had heard that same term somewhere else recently. . . . I remembered where I had heard it, *The Shack*.

> Beginning in chapter 9 in *The Shack*, which is titled, "A Long Time Ago in a Garden Far, Far Away," . . . Sarayu (who represents the Holy Spirit) has created a garden and we learn that the garden is a fractal. We learn about fractals from Sarayu when she says, "A fractal is something considered simple and orderly that is actually composed of repeated patterns no matter how magnified. A fractal is almost infinitely complex. I love fractals, so I put them everywhere."[35]

Curious about the term "fractal" that was showing up in both *The Shack* and *The Seeker*, the young woman had done some research. What she discovered is that the term "fractal" is directly related to what are being called the "new sciences" of "Chaos Theory" and "Fractal Theory." What was of particular interest to me was her finding that fractals are directly linked with the occult phrase "as above, so below." Given my previously expressed concern about Peterson's use of "as above, so below" in *The Message*, I found it interesting that "as above, so below" was apparently related to the term fractal in *The Shack*.

As Above, So Below and Fractals

After reading the article, I made sure a copy was sent to my friend Pastor Larry DeBruyn. Because he had been currently writing articles exposing *The Shack's* errant theology, I knew he would be interested in her article—how she had discovered a direct link between *The Shack's* multiple references to fractals and the New Age term "as above, so below."[36]

Later, as we talked by phone, Larry searched the Internet for the word "fractal." The first website listed was called *Fractal Wisdom.* The site featured an article titled "Fractal Chaos Crashes the Wall between Science and Religion."[37] Under that heading was a box containing a fractal design, and underneath the fractal was the saying "As Above, So Below." Underneath the occult saying was a quote from New Age pioneer and mystic Aldous Huxley—the single most quoted person in Marilyn Ferguson's best-selling New Age book *The Aquarian Conspiracy.* Huxley is also quoted by Rick Warren in *The Purpose Driven Life.*[38] Huxley's quote on the *Fractal Wisdom* website addresses the dual subjects of chaos and "purpose":

> At any given moment, life is completely senseless. But viewed over a period, it seems to reveal itself as an organism existing in time, having a purpose, trending in a certain direction.[39]

The online article titled "Fractal Chaos Crashes the Wall Between Science and Religion" goes on to state:

> New discoveries in the science and mathematics of Chaos research are revolutionizing our world view. They reveal a hidden fractal order underlying all seemingly chaotic events. The fractals are intricate and beautiful. They repeat basic patterns, but with an infinity of variations and forms. The world-view emerging

from this scientific research is new, and yet at the same time ancient. With a little thought, and the help of this web, you can better understand the significance of Chaos and Fractals. You can see how to use these insights in your life to create a bridge between Science and Spirituality.[40]

As the mystic sages of long ago put it, "as above, so below."[41]

But what is being presented as "science" is actually an occult/New Age worldview, which presents the New Age belief that much of the "chaos" in the world is the result of people not properly perceiving the "interconnectedness" of all things. In other words, what appears to be "chaos" is often just "the observer" not seeing the "as above, so below"/God "in" everything/"fractal order" that defines all creation. This postulated fractal order is directly related to the teachings of Teilhard de Chardin, Matthew Fox, and Leonard Sweet. *The Shack*'s references to fractals—references I had overlooked when I first read the book—immediately explain why author William Paul Young capitalizes the letter "C" in the word "Creation" at least twenty times in *The Shack*. The capital "C" reflects what his "Jesus" is teaching—that God is "in" all things—including "Creation."

From the perspective of the New Age/New Gospel/New Spirituality, it makes perfect sense that the "Jesus" of *The Shack* states that God is "in" all things. Mack—the main character—is seeing his life as "a mess" rather than as a "fractal" part of "God." This is because he is not seeing the "as above, so below" fractal order of "God in all things." From this perspective, it also makes perfect sense that *The Shack*'s "Holy Spirit" told Mack that his life only seems chaotic and "a mess"—that in reality, he was actually "a living fractal."[42]

Fractal Wisdom?

Also, from the *Fractal Wisdom* website, I could see the deceptive New Age ploy regarding the word fractal and its relationship to "as above, so below." If all of capital "C" Creation is "God" and thus composed of "God" atoms and energy, then any fractal part of Creation is therefore a part of God. Man is a fractal. Man is God. That is why Mack is told he is "a living fractal." That is why Mack is told that God is "in" all things.[43] The word fractal is being used as a pseudo-scientific synonym for the belief that God is "in" everything—everything being a fractal or a fractured part of the whole, a fractured part of God. Taken a step further, *The Shack* is indirectly presenting the notion that "chaos" is simply the result of people not seeing the "God in everything" fractal order in the world—"as above, so below."

Thus, *The Shack* subtly introduces the New Age/New Spirituality as a worldview that puts forth the notion that "chaos" can be significantly overcome when humanity stops seeing itself as "separate"[44] but rather sees itself as "One"—as a part of the "God" who is "in" everyone and everything. However, the Bible teaches that humanity is not "God" or "One" with God (John 2:24-25; Ezekiel 28:2; Hosea 11:9, etc.). The Bible teaches just the opposite—that man is actually separated from God by sin (Isaiah 59:2). It is because of this separation that we need to acknowledge our sin and repent (Acts 2:38). Everyone must be born again (John 3:6-7)—born again from the God who is "above" (John 3:31), and not "below." Born again from the one true God—not by the "as above, so below" god that the apostle Paul described as "the god of this world" (2 Corinthians 4:4). The Bible states that we are only "one" *in* Christ Jesus (Galatians 3:28). And we are only "one" in Christ Jesus when we repent of our sins and accept His death on the cross for our sins (1 John 2:2)—His finished work on the cross of Calvary (Colossians 1:20).

"Chaos" is not created or furthered by humanity's denial of its so-called fractal divinity. Rather, "chaos" is the consequence of Adam's fall resulting in sinfulness and the subsequent decay of all things and our separation from a holy God. It is not "as above, so below." Fractals do not point the way to salvation. As cited, the Bible warns about a deceptive and spiritually dangerous imagined Oneness:

> And the LORD said, Behold, the people is one, and they have all one language; and this they begin to do: and now nothing will be restrained from them, which they have imagined to do. (Genesis 11:6)

One Blood But Not One Spirit

Acts 17:26 informs us that humanity is "one blood" and that we are connected to one another in that physical way. But humanity is *not* one Spirit. "That which is born of the flesh is flesh; and that which is born of the Spirit is spirit" (John 3:6). The Bible states that "flesh and blood cannot inherit the kingdom of God" (1 Corinthians 15:50). Jesus said, we "must be born again" (John 3:7).

God's creation is indeed intricate and wondrous. And in many countless ways it is beautifully and harmoniously interconnected—but it is not divine (Romans 1:25). Man is "fearfully and wonderfully made" (Psalm 139:14), but he is not a part of some divine fractal order. We are sinners, and we need to be saved from the sin that separates us from God. It is as simple as that. Repenting and accepting Jesus Christ as our Lord and as the one and only Savior who saves us from our sins is the "narrow" and only way to eternal salvation (John 14:6; Matthew 7:13-14). The introduction of fractals in the story line of *The Shack* is a deceptive device that seduces unsuspecting readers into a universalistic quantum spirituality. It is an entry point into the pseudo-scientific notion of "fractal Oneness"—"as above, so below"/God "in" everything.

The Shack may seem "wonderful" to countless *Shack* readers, but in reality it is a betrayal of biblical Christianity and of our Lord and Savior Jesus Christ. In the words of the prophet Jeremiah—*The Shack* may seem "wonderful," but it is actually "horrible," and yet the people "love to have it so."

> A wonderful and horrible thing is committed in the land; The prophets prophesy falsely, and the priests bear rule by their means; and my people love to have it so: and what will ye do in the end thereof? (Jeremiah 5:30-31)

For if he that cometh preacheth another Jesus, whom we have not preached, or if ye receive another spirit, which ye have not received, or another gospel, which ye have not accepted, ye might well bear with him. (2 Corinthians 11:4)

7

The New Age Implications
of *Jesus Calling*

In *"Another Jesus" Calling*, I describe many problems regarding Sarah Young's best-selling book *Jesus Calling*. In particular, there are some serious New Age implications to what her "Jesus" is presenting in his "messages" to Young and her countless readers. Nevertheless, Laura Minchew, a Senior Vice-President at Thomas Nelson publishers, adamantly defends *Jesus Calling* and defiantly denies that the book has any New Age implications. She told *World Net Daily*, "I will tell you that should anyone hint of New Age teachings in *Jesus Calling*, they would be sorely misinformed."[1]

But Minchew's statement is both ironic and untrue. It is ironic because even as she was issuing her denial, Thomas Nelson editors were busy deleting some of the very New Age material in question. I'm not sure what Laura Minchew's understanding of the New Age is, but as a former New Ager, I can assure you there are many New Age implications—both direct and indirect—in *Jesus Calling*. The following are ten of them.

New Age Implications: Ten Examples

I. The New Age Book *God Calling*

In an interview with the Christian Broadcasting Network, Sarah Young said she was inspired to receive direct messages from "Jesus" after reading the book *God Calling*. She stated:

> My journey began with a devotional book (*God Calling*) written in the 1930s by two women who practiced waiting in God's Presence, writing the messages they received as they "listened." About a year after I started reading this book, I began to wonder if I too could receive messages during my times of communing with God. . . . So I decided to "listen" to God with pen in hand, writing down whatever I sensed He was saying.[2]

Unfortunately, Sarah Young and her Thomas Nelson editors missed the fact that *God Calling* is a channeled New Age book. The "messages" received by the two women appear to be legitimate to the undiscerning reader because they are presented in the form of a daily devotional. Ironically, *God Calling* could have been titled *Jesus Calling* because its messages were reputedly dictated by "The Living Christ Himself."[3] It is worth noting that *Jesus Calling* is similarly titled and similarly presents its reputed "messages" from "Jesus" in the form of a daily devotional.

In *The Encyclopedia of New Age Beliefs* published by Harvest House Christian publishers, authors John Weldon and John Ankerberg provide ample evidence as to why *God Calling* is a channeled New Age book. In their chapter on channeling—under the subheading of "Impersonations and Denials of Christianity"—the two respected apologists describe *God Calling* as a book "replete with denials of biblical teaching"[4] as it "subtly encourages psychic development and spiritistic inspiration under the guise of Christ's personal guidance . . . and often misinterprets Scripture."[5] Citing a number of passages in *God Calling* that are unbiblical and have New Age implications, the two authors explain that channeling is a form of occult mediumship and according to the Bible "is a practice specifically forbidden (Deuteronomy 18:9-12)."[6] Yet Sarah Young stated it was *God Calling* that inspired her to receive her own "messages" from "Jesus." In her original introduction to *Jesus Calling*, Young went out of her way to praise *God Calling* as "a treasure to me."[7] Sadly, her lofty endorsement greatly popularized this New Age book within mainstream Christianity. As a result, *God Calling* was commonly found in great numbers in various editions in both secular and Christian bookstores. In fact, it was often shelved alongside *Jesus Calling*.

Note: Young's response to the valid criticism that *Jesus Calling* had been inspired by a channeled New Age book, was to quickly remove all references to *God Calling* from all the new printings of *Jesus Calling*. No explanations. No apologies. No anything. Like the missing 18½ minutes from Richard Nixon's Watergate tapes, *God Calling* has disappeared from the pages of Young's book.

II. Channeled "Messages" from "Jesus"

Ruth Graham, writing about *Jesus Calling* in *The Daily Beast*—a popular online news organization formerly associated with *Newsweek* magazine—reported that Thomas Nelson had specifically requested that she not use the word "channeling" to describe how Sarah Young was receiving her "messages" from "Jesus." Graham wrote:

> Thomas Nelson specifically requested I not use the word "channeling" to describe Young's first-person writing in the voice of Jesus—the word has New Age connotations—but it's hard to avoid it in describing the book's rhetorical approach.[8]

In *Jesus Calling*, Young writes that "Jesus" told her "to be a channel of My loving Presence."[9] Obliging his request, her book is filled with channeled "messages" and "directives" she claims to have received from God. In her original 2004 introduction, she wrote:

> I have continued to receive *personal messages from God* as I meditate on Him. The more difficult my life circumstances, the more I need these *encouraging directives from my Creator.*[10] (emphasis added)

Regarding this type of spiritualism, *Webster's New World Dictionary* defines the word "channel" as follows: "to serve as a medium for (a spirit)."[11] It defines the word "directive" as "a general instruction or order issued authoritatively."[12] And by Sarah Young's own description in her original introduction, this is exactly what she is doing—being "a channel" for "encouraging directives" from a spiritual "Presence" that presents itself as "Jesus." After receiving these "messages" and "directives," she arranged them in the form of a daily devotional—just like *God Calling*.

Note: The paragraph cited above—where Young originally described how she has "continued to receive personal messages from God" and "encouraging directives" from her "Creator"—has been completely removed from the new editions of *Jesus Calling*.[13]

III. Visualization

Sarah Young engaged in the occult/New Age practice of "visualization" when she "pictured" her family "encircled by God's protective Presence":

> One morning as I prayed, *I visualized* God protecting each of us. *I pictured* first our daughter, then our son, and then Steve encircled by God's protective Presence, which looked like golden light. When I prayed for myself, I was suddenly enveloped in brilliant light and profound peace. I lost all sense of time as I experienced God's Presence in this powerful way.[14] (emphasis added)

In the same *Encyclopedia of New Age Beliefs* that described *God Calling* as a channeled New Age book, a specific chapter on visualization warns about the spiritual dangers of this New Age practice:

> "Visualization" and "guided imagery" have long been recognized by sorcerers of all kinds as the most powerful and effective methodology for contacting the spirit world in order to acquire supernatural power, knowledge, and healing. Such methods are neither taught nor practiced in the Bible as helps to faith or prayer.[15]

Sarah Young just assumed that the "light" she visualized enveloping her family and herself was from God. But one cannot assume anything in regard to spiritual experiences and spiritual encounters—especially when engaging in the occult practice of visualization. Because "many false prophets are gone out into the world," we are told to "try the spirits" to see "whether they are of God" (1 John 4:1). The apostle Paul warned of deceptive "seducing spirits" (1 Timothy 4:1) and how Satan can come as "an angel of light" (2 Corinthians 11:14). Also, Jesus specifically warned us to beware of a light that appears to be light but is actually darkness (Luke 11:35).

Note: Recent editions of *Jesus Calling* have attempted to subtly demystify Sarah Young's mystical New Age "prayer" process. The phrase "looked like golden light" and the trance-like sentence "I lost all sense of time as I experienced God's Presence in this powerful way" have both been deleted from recent editions of *Jesus Calling*.[16]

IV. Meditation

Jesus Calling readers are led to equate Sarah Young's contemplative prayer process with biblical meditation. But to "make your mind like a still pool of water" as you passively wait "to receive whatever thoughts" Young's "Jesus" may "drop into it" is much more akin to Eastern/New Age meditation. Biblical meditation, if you will, is an active attentiveness and thinking upon Scripture. Eastern/New Age meditation is more subjective and open to spiritual suggestion. In his August 5th message, Sarah Young's "Jesus" promotes this New Age form of meditation and contemplative prayer:

> Make your mind like a still pool of water, ready to receive whatever thoughts I drop into it.[17]

Stilling and quieting one's mind may seem to be peaceful and godly, but passively stilling the mind (i.e., putting the mind in neutral) can provide an opening for seducing spirits to communicate with an undiscerning meditator—all in the name of "Jesus," "God," and the "Holy Spirit" (Ephesians 4:27, 1 Timothy 4:1, 2 Corinthians 11:4). Sarah Young describes how she receives these "thoughts" as "messages" and "directives" as she meditates on "Jesus":

> I have continued to receive personal messages from God as I meditate on Him. The more difficult my life circumstances, the more I need these encouraging directives from my Creator.[18]

But this kind of spiritual activity is not scriptural, and it is not biblical meditation. This is Eastern/New Age meditation. This type of meditation is what New Age channelers do to make contact with the spirit world.

Note: It bears repeating that the above paragraph containing the words "meditate," "messages," and "directives" has been deleted from recent editions of *Jesus Calling*.

V. New Age Terminology

Throughout *Jesus Calling*, Sarah Young's "Jesus" casually introduces New Age terminology in his channeled messages. Not that long ago terms like co-create,[19] divine alchemy,[20] Love-Light,[21] Light-bearer,[22] supernatural plane,[23] living channel,[24] paradigm shift,[25] true self,[26] ultimate reality,[27] universal presence,[28] etc., were sure indicators of someone's metaphysical/New Age orientation. But now these terms are commonly found in "Christian" books like *Jesus Calling* and are rapidly becoming part of the everyday language of the church.

Sarah Young's "Jesus" also makes indirect reference to two of the mega best-selling New Age books of the last thirty years—Shirley MacLaine's *Out on a Limb* and M. Scott Peck's *The Road Less Traveled*. Young's "Jesus" invites her millions of readers to "go out on a limb" with him and to take "a road less traveled":

> Be willing to go out on a limb with Me.[29]

> You, however, have been called to take a "road less traveled."[30]

Note: Obviously, these two phrases can be used in other contexts. However, the true Jesus Christ is quite aware of these groundbreaking New Age books, and it defies reason that He would make any reference—direct or indirect—to these hugely popular metaphysical books. God is not the author of confusion (1 Corinthians 14:33). And He is not going to introduce anything that might stumble someone—like nonchalantly referring to two New Age books that have already stumbled the millions of people who have read them and been influenced by them. (1 Corinthians 8:9).

VI. Divine Alchemy

Regarding other overlapping New Age terminology in *Jesus Calling*, Sarah Young's "Jesus" states:

> I can glean Joy out of sorrow, Peace out of adversity. Only a Friend who is also the King of kings could accomplish this divine alchemy.[31]

However, the term "divine alchemy" is an ancient, mystical, occult/New Age term that raises multiple spiritual concerns. The word "occult" is defined in *Webster's New World Dictionary* as follows:

> . . . designating or of certain alleged mystic arts, such as magic, *alchemy,* astrology, etc.[32] (emphasis added)

The *Oxford Classical Dictionary* underscores the fact that the "art" of alchemy has serious New Age implications. The very first sentence of the definition states:

> *Alchemy* in antiquity was a mixture of chemical, metallurgical, and glass technology, Greek philosophy, *mystical and syncretist religion, and astrology.*[33] (emphasis added)

The same *Oxford Dictionary* explains the occult/New Age underpinnings of alchemy itself:

> The art is distinguished from the pure science of chemistry by its mixture of *mystical and magical elements* with the technology . . . Alchemy in late antiquity was born of the confluence of three streams: (1) technology . . . (2) theory . . . (3) *occult religion.*[34] (emphasis added)

By Googling divine alchemy on the Internet, one will see countless references to the occult. The term divine alchemy is frequently found in the teachings of New Age leaders such as Marianne Williamson. She uses the term divine alchemy to reference the same practice of meditation Sarah Young's "Jesus" is advocating. She writes:

> Meditation is time spent with God in silence and quiet listening. It is the time during which the Holy Spirit has a chance to enter into our minds and perform His *divine alchemy.*[35] (emphasis added)

The *Oxford Classical Dictionary* further describes the origin of alchemy and how it is linked to other occult sciences:

> The inventor was said to be Hermes [Trismegistus], and *alchemy is linked with other occult sciences* in the Hermetic literature of the first three centuries A.D., along with neo-Pythagorean, Neoplatonic, and Gnostic ideas.[36] (emphasis added)

Note: Once again, it is inconceivable that the true Jesus Christ would ever use a term like divine alchemy that is so highly identified with the occult. This is yet one more troublesome New Age aspect to *Jesus Calling* and one more reason to question the authenticity of Sarah Young's "Jesus."

VII. Co-creation

Sarah Young's "Jesus" also introduces the key New Age concept of "co-creation." This is a New Age evolutionary concept that falsely teaches that because man is God, he can therefore co-create with God. But man is not God.

The false New Age "Christ" has a plan. He is promising the world that Armageddon can be avoided and world peace can be achieved if everyone collaborates and "co-creates" with him. Speaking through top New Age leader Barbara Marx Hubbard in her book *The Revelation*, the New Age "Christ" uses the terms co-create, co-creation, co-creative, co-creator, and co-creatorship over 100 times. This is because co-creation is a key element in the New Age Christ's counterfeit plan of salvation for Planet Earth. At one point Hubbard's "Christ" states:

> Here we are, now poised either on the brink of destruction greater than the world has ever seen—a destruction which will cripple planet Earth forever and release only the few to go on—or on the threshold of *global co-creation* wherein

each person on Earth will be attracted to participate in his or her own evolution to godliness.[37] (emphasis added)

New Age author Neale Donald Walsch has been taking spiritual dictation from his New Age "God" for many years now. Soon after the tragic events of September 11th, 2001, "God," speaking through Walsch, proclaimed that "the era of the Single Savior is over." He said:

> Yet let me make something clear. *The era of the Single Savior is over.* What is needed now is joint action, combined effort, collective *co-creation.*[38] (emphasis added)

In *Jesus Calling*, Young's "Jesus" introduces the idea of co-creation in conjunction with the term "collaborating." *Webster's New World Dictionary's* sole definition of a collaborationist is "a person who cooperates with an enemy invader."[39] Sarah Young's "Jesus" plays right into this New Age collaboration when he talks of humanity collaborating and co-creating with him:

> This is a very practical way of *collaborating* with Me. I, the Creator of the universe, have deigned to *co-create* with you.[40] (emphasis added)

Co-creation is a crucial New Age concept that entails the necessity of man recognizing he is God and then acting as God to affirm, visualize, envision, and to ultimately co-create with God a positive peaceful future. Thus, there is a definite overlap of terms as Sarah Young's "Jesus" similarly teaches that humanity can partner with God through the co-creation process.

The New Age "Christ" refers to a future world peace that can be visualized and *co-created* by mankind. This co-created world peace is referred to as the "alternative to Armageddon."[41] But the Bible warns that what will one day seem to be a time of peace and safety will end in destruction (1 Thessalonians 5:3).

Note: This "alternative to Armageddon" peace process is described by New Age leaders as an important part of "God's Dream" for the world. Not surprisingly, "God's Dream" is another New Age concept that is introduced in *Jesus Calling*.

VIII. "God's Dream"

Consistent with many of the other New Age implications contained in her channeled messages, Sarah Young's "Jesus" introduces the New Age idea of "God's Dream" in *Jesus Calling* when he states:

> I may infuse within you a dream that seems far beyond your reach.[42]

In *Jesus Calling: 365 Devotions for Kids*, the January 6th message/devotion has "Jesus" telling the children:

Dare to Dream My Dream.[43]

The term "God's Dream" is yet another part of the overlapping New Age language streaming into the church. "God's Dream" is a vague, loosely defined New Age metaphor that attempts to unify different religions and faith groups in an unbiblical effort to attain world peace. However, the true Jesus Christ warned that deception and the coming of Antichrist—not a "God's Dream" peace movement—will be what actually precedes His ultimate and glorious return (Matthew 24:3-5; 2 Thessalonians 2:1-5).

The prophet Daniel warned that Antichrist will "destroy wonderfully" and "by peace shall destroy many" (Daniel 8:24-25). In the future, what may appear to be a "wonderful" worldwide revival and a "wonderful" world peace will actually be a false revival and a false peace—the kind of false peace that Daniel warned would be associated with the coming of Antichrist, not the true Christ.

As cited, the New Age concept of "God's Dream" was introduced at least as far back as 1904 by New Age theosophists in their *New*

Century Path magazine.[44] Since then it has been used by numerous New Age sympathizers that include Oprah Winfrey,[45] Wayne Dyer,[46] former United Nations Indian guru Sri Chinmoy,[47] and African bishop Desmond Tutu.[48] Also as cited, the New Age concept of "God's Dream" was introduced into the church in the 1970s by former Crystal Cathedral pastor Robert Schuller[49] and later adopted by Rick Warren,[50] Brian McLaren,[51] Joel Osteen,[52] Bruce Wilkinson,[53] Leonard Sweet,[54] and many other Christian figures. The overlap factor is very apparent when comparing statements made by Oprah Winfrey, Joel Osteen, and Sarah Young's "Jesus":

- **Oprah Winfrey:** God can dream a bigger dream for you than you can dream for yourself.[55]

- **Joel Osteen:** God's dream for your life is so much bigger than your own.[56]

- **Sarah Young's "Jesus":** Dream your biggest, most incredible dream—and then know that I am able to do far more than that, far more than you can ever ask or imagine. Allow Me to fill your mind with My dreams for you.[57]

Rick Warren, Brian McLaren, and Leonard Sweet all used the "God's Dream" metaphor to stress the urgency of achieving world peace—but at what compromised New Age cost?

- **Rick Warren:** This weekend, I'll begin a series of five messages on God's dream to use you globally—to literally use YOU to help change the world! I'll unveil our Global P.E.A.C.E. plan, and how God has uniquely prepared you for this moment of destiny.[58]

- **Brian McLaren:** That in itself is an act of peacemaking, because we're seeking to align our wills with God's will, our dreams with God's dream.[59]

• **Leonard Sweet:** The time to save God's Dream is now. The People to save God's Dream are you.[60]

"God's Dream" Is a False Dream

"God's Dream" may *seem* to be inspirational and have a godly feel to it, but there is nothing in Scripture to even hint, much less substantiate, the New Age concept of "God's Dream." God doesn't dream in any way, shape, manner, or form. "God's Dream" is definitely one of those crossover terms like "co-creation" and "divine alchemy" that attempt to "shift" everything into a New Age context and towards the universal acceptance of a New Age/New Worldview. Sarah Young's "Jesus" plays right into this clever conditioning when he introduces the concept of "God's Dream" in *Jesus Calling* and in no less than three of Sarah Young's other books.[61] The prophet Jeremiah warned about those who prophesy and present false dreams like "God's Dream" (Jeremiah 23:32).

Note: Because so many Christian leaders have adopted the concept of "God's Dream," it has become a popularly accepted "Christian" term and is now virtually indistinguishable from its New Age origins.

IX. God "in" Everything

The New Age teaches we are all "One" and we are all "God" because God is "in" everyone and everything. As cited, this panentheistic belief is the foundational teaching of the New Age movement. But the true Jesus Christ never taught that God is "in" everything. Yet the July 8th "message" that Sarah Young said she received from her "Jesus" definitely presents this false New Age teaching:

I am above all, as well as in all . . . [62]

However, the true Jesus Christ would never teach that God is "in all" as Sarah Young's "Jesus" states in *Jesus Calling*.

Note: Yet many Scriptures refute this idea that God is "in" all—Ezekiel 28:2, Galatians 6:3, Psalm 9:20, Isaiah 31:3, John 2:24-25, etc. Psalm 39:5 makes it very clear that "every man at his best state is altogether vanity." Man is not God or a part of God because God is not universally "in" everything—God is not "in all."

X. Sarah Young's New Agey Mystical Moonlight Conversion

In the original introduction to *Jesus Calling*, Sarah Young described how it was a walk in "God's glorious creation" that led to her mystical moonlight conversion—that her "heart" was "converted" to "Jesus" when she "felt" "enveloped" by the "warm mist" of His "Presence." Her account is reminiscent of how many of us fell prey to deceptive spiritual experiences rather than heeding warnings from the Word of God about "another Jesus," "another gospel," and "another spirit" (2 Corinthians 11:4; Galatians 1:6-7; 1 Timothy 4:1). Notice how Young clearly transitions from "it was God's glorious creation that helped me open my heart to Him" right into her walk in the "snowy mountains" with its "cold moonlit beauty." In her initial introduction there was a continuous flow from one paragraph to the next. I use italics to indicate the New Agey references Young removed from the original introduction. She wrote:

> It was the intellectual integrity of Francis Schaeffer's teaching that had drawn me to that pristine place. Though the quest that had taken me there was a search for truth, *it was God's glorious creation that helped me open my heart to Him.*

> One night I found myself leaving the warmth of our cozy chalet to walk alone in the snowy mountains. I went into a deeply wooded area, feeling vulnerable and awed by cold, moonlit beauty. The air was crisp and dry, piercing to inhale. *Suddenly I felt as if a warm mist enveloped me.* I became aware of a lovely Presence, and my involuntary response was to whisper, "Sweet Jesus." *This utterance was*

totally uncharacteristic of me, and I was shocked to hear myself speaking so tenderly to Jesus. As I pondered this brief communication, I realized it was the response of a converted heart; at that moment I knew I belonged to Him. This was far more than the intellectual answers for which I'd been searching. This was a relationship with the Creator of the universe. [63]

New Conversion Account

But after nine years of publishing the mystical conversion account above, this original version was suddenly replaced by a different, more traditional conversion account that Young now claims to have had prior to her moonlight walk. Instead of "God's glorious creation" transitioning into her mystical moonlight conversion, now it's her new conversion account that transitions into her considerably toned-down walk in the moonlight. The new account reads:

Shortly after I settled into the home I shared with other students, I met a gifted counselor who had come from the Swiss branch of L'Abri to talk with some of us. I went into the room where she was waiting, and she told me to close the door. Before I even had time to sit down, she asked her first question: "Are you a Christian?" I answered that I wasn't sure; I wanted to be a Christian, but I didn't really understand why I needed Jesus. I thought that knowing God might be enough. Her second question was: "What can you not forgive yourself for?" This question brought me face-to-face with my sinfulness, and immediately I understood my need for Jesus—to save me from my many sins. Later, when I was alone, I asked Him to forgive all my sins and to be my Savior-God.

One night I found myself leaving the warmth of our cozy chalet to walk alone in the snowy mountains. I went into a deeply wooded area, feeling vulnerable and awed by cold, moonlit beauty. The air was crisp and dry, piercing to inhale. After a while, I came into an open area and I stopped walking. Time seemed to stand still as I gazed around me in wonder—soaking in the beauty of this place. Suddenly I became aware of a lovely Presence with me, and my involuntary response was to whisper, "Sweet Jesus." This experience of Jesus' Presence was far more personal than the intellectual answers for which I'd been searching. This was a relationship with the Creator of the universe—the One who is the way, the truth, and the life.[64]

This new conversion account immediately begs the question of why Young didn't include this later conversion account in her original writing. For nine years she described how her "heart" was "converted" in the "cold moonlit beauty" of "God's glorious creation." Now we are being told that her heart was converted previous to her walk in the moonlight after talking with a L'Abri counselor.

Note: The skeptical reader might see how the author is attempting to do some quick damage control—especially in light of the fact that a number of the controversial statements from her original conversion account have been completely deleted from the most recent editions of *Jesus Calling*. Gone is the original statement that transitioned to her mystical conversion—"it was God's glorious creation that helped me open my heart to Him." Gone is the "warm mist" that "enveloped" her. Gone is the "utterance" that was "totally uncharacteristic of me." Gone is her being "shocked" to hear herself "speaking so tenderly to Jesus." Gone is her realization that her "response" was that of "a converted heart." Gone is "at that moment I knew I belonged to Him." More succinctly—gone is her whole mystical moonlight conversion and gone are most of the New Age implications of what she actually experienced. Also gone for many of us is any real credibility for an author and publisher who are trying to edit their problems away without any explanation or apology to anyone—much less the millions of readers who read her original version.

Conclusion

It seems a bit disingenuous for Thomas Nelson Vice President Laura Minchew to deny the many New Age implications of *Jesus Calling*—even as they are deleting much of the very material that substantiates the New Age implications charge. Like an octopus that shoots ink at its perceived adversaries to cloud the waters, Minchew's attempt to intimidate critics and to dispel legitimate criticism is not credible. Laura Minchew, Sarah Young, and Thomas Nelson editors must know this or they wouldn't be removing so much controversial material from their new editions of *Jesus Calling*.

When the author and her Thomas Nelson team choose to protect their multi-million-dollar *Jesus Calling* industry rather than the truth, they betray the countless readers who have put their trust in Sarah Young's "Jesus." Nevertheless, some will still say—"but there is so much truth and so much Scripture, and I was so encouraged by Sarah Young's book." Or, "Hey, so what if they changed things. They were just trying to make it right—so what's the problem? But it is a sad day when avowed Christians find themselves encouraged by a deceptive mix of truth and New Age error. And when an author and a publisher make significant changes to spiritually controversial material, they should provide some kind of explanation as to why those changes were made.

This much is for sure. The true Christ doesn't mix truth with New Age teachings. This is what a false Christ does. When asked by His disciples what would be the sign of His coming and the end of the world, the true Jesus Christ said that deception would be the sign—that many would come in His name and pretend to be Him (Matthew 24:3-5). And while this might be hard for some people to accept, His warning specifically applies to false Christs like Sarah Young's "Jesus."

> Beloved, believe not every spirit, but try the spirits whether they are of God: because many false prophets are gone out into the world. (1 John 4:1)

Then if any man shall say unto you, Lo, here is Christ, or there; believe it not. (Matthew 24:23)

A False New Age Christ– What We Can Learn

Maitreya

On April 25,1982, a number of major newspapers around the world carried a prominent full-page ad announcing that "the Christ" was here on Earth waiting for humanity to call him forth. However, these ads made it very clear that his name was Lord Maitreya—not Jesus Christ. The ads headlined, "THE CHRIST IS NOW HERE. HOW WILL WE RECOGNIZE HIM?" and proclaimed:

> Look for a modern man concerned with modern problems—political, economic, and social. Since July, 1977, the Christ has been emerging as a spokesman for a group or community in a well-known modern country. He is not a religious leader, but an educator in the broadest sense of the word—pointing the way out of our present crisis. We will recognize Him by His extraordinary spiritual potency, the universality of His viewpoint, and His love for all humanity. He comes not to judge, but to aid and inspire.

The ads continued, "WHO IS THE CHRIST?," stating:

> Throughout history, humanity's evolution has been guided by a group of enlightened men, the Masters of Wisdom. They have remained largely in the remote desert and mountain places of earth, working mainly through their disciples who live openly in the world. . . . At the center of this "Spiritual Hierarchy" stands the World Teacher, *Lord Maitreya,* known by Christians as the *Christ.* And as Christians await the Second Coming, so the Jews await the *Messiah,* the Buddhists the fifth *Buddha,* the Moslims the *Imam Mahdi,* and the Hindus await *Krishna.* These are all names for one individual.[1]

This stunning announcement sent shock waves throughout the civilized world, but those who read and understood their Bibles knew that Maitreya was not the true Christ. Yet one thing was for sure—Maitreya's followers were very serious about what they were doing. They managed the Share International worldwide organization that promoted Maitreya's teachings with main offices in London, Tokyo, Amsterdam, and Los Angeles.

Today, some forty years after those 1982 newspaper ads, Share International still professes Maitreya's presence in the world. This false New Age Christ has never gone away as he purports to wait for a beleaguered humanity to call him forth from his present anonymity. Yet given his decades-old insistence that he is "the Christ" and given his devoted following, there is an inexplicable silence in the Christian church regarding the subject of Maitreya.

For whatever reasons, Christian leaders have never taken Maitreya or his New Age teachings seriously. Focused on almost everything except protecting the flock, most pastors and church leaders remain unconcerned or just plain ignorant about Maitreya and the New Age in general. For them, Maitreya and the New Age are more than passe—just simply fads that came and went. Consequently, most Christians today have no idea how the world is being methodically prepared to accept a false New Age Christ—someone like Maitreya.

Prototype? Antichrist?

Maitreya's teachings are amazingly consistent with a New Age/New Gospel/New Spirituality that seeks to become the foundation for a New World Religion. This is one of the chief reasons someone like Maitreya serves not only as a possible prototype for Antichrist but remains a viable candidate for the position himself.

Over the years, Maitreya maintained contact with the world through his longtime chief spokesperson, the late British author, artist, esotericist, and New Age channeler, Benjamin Creme (1922-2016). Maitreya's role as the alleged "Christ" was introduced by Creme in his 1980 book, *The Reappearance of the Christ and the Masters of Wisdom*. Another Maitreya spokesperson—the late Wayne S. Peterson (1941-2017)—wrote a 2001 book titled *Extraordinary Times, Extraordinary Beings: Experiences of an American Diplomat with Maitreya and the Masters of Wisdom*. Peterson, a former U.S. government diplomat, corroborated what Creme had taught while adding anecdotes and experiences of his own—including two personal encounters he claims to have had with Maitreya.

Both Creme and Peterson describe how Maitreya's purpose is to teach humanity that we are all "One" because God is "in" everyone and everything. And because we are all said to be "One," we must learn to live in "right relationship" as brothers and sisters in our "One" great family. The first step in recognizing this Oneness is to establish "sharing" as the way to eliminate poverty and starvation in the world. Thus, Maitreya is "emerging" as the "World Teacher" to teach us how to save ourselves and save our planet and how, when enough people call him forth, he will finally reveal himself in an internationally televised "Day of Declaration."[2]

Through the years, Benjamin Creme traveled the world giving lectures in Western and Eastern Europe, Japan, Australia,

New Zealand, Canada, Mexico, and the United States—often to large crowds in popular venues like San Francisco's Masonic Auditorium and Palace of Fine Arts. He was widely interviewed on international radio and television. In his many books, lectures, interviews, and posts on the Share International website, Creme described how Maitreya materialized in spiritual gatherings around the world—sometimes taking on the form of a messianic figure recognizable to that culture. Most notable was his appearance in Nairobi, Kenya in 1988 where he was said to be identified as "the Christ" in front of 6,000 people.[3] Maitreya's followers have reportedly been numbered among many prominent figures that include the late former Russian Premier Mikhail Gorbachev[4] and the late African leader Nelson Mandela.[5]

Curiously, British Indian-American academic, journalist, activist, and author Raj Patel was brought forward in 2010 as a possible candidate for being the otherwise incognito Maitreya.[6] Described by one source as the "rock star of social justice writing,"[7] Patel, ironically, had some distinct qualifying characteristics that Creme had described as being unique to Maitreya. While speculation about Patel being Maitreya faded after both Benjamin Creme and Raj Patel issued seeming denials, Patel remains part of the ongoing mystique surrounding this false New Age Christ.

Maitreya's "Master Jesus" Ploy

For if he that cometh preacheth another Jesus, whom we have not preached, or if ye receive another spirit, which ye have not received, or another gospel, which ye have not accepted, ye might well bear with him. (2 Corinthians 11:4)

The whole "Master Jesus" deception bears repeating. In what would be a cunning counterfeit of the Bible's description of the return of Jesus with his "mighty angels" (2 Thessalonians 1:7), Maitreya states that when he reveals himself as "the Christ," twelve "Masters of Wisdom" will appear with him. They will work together to teach humanity his *New Truth*[8] and his *New Way*[9] for the coming *New Age*.[10] One of these spiritual "Masters" returning with him is said to be the enlightened "Master Jesus"—who is not Jesus Christ—but is presented as a "disciple" of "the Christ"—Maitreya. It is made clear that Maitreya is the only person occupying the "Office" of "Christ" and that he has occupied this "Office" for over 2600 years. Reputedly, it was Maitreya as "Christ" who overshadowed and worked through the man Jesus in Palestine back in the first century. Benjamin Creme explained:

> In the esoteric tradition, the Christ is not the name of an individual but of an Office in the Hierarchy. The present holder of that Office, the Lord Maitreya, has held it for 2,600 years, and manifested in Palestine through His Disciple, Jesus, by the occult method of overshadowing, the most frequent form used for the manifestation of Avatars. He has never left the world, but for 2,000 years has waited and planned for this immediate future time, training His Disciples, and preparing Himself for the awesome task which awaits Him. He has made it known that this time, He Himself will come.[11]

Thus, Maitreya's "Master Jesus" is not described as Lord and Christ. Rather, he is described as a "Master" and a "Master" only. Maitreya says it is *he himself* who is Lord and Christ. Creme explains that the "Master Jesus" will be serving the "Lord" and "Christ" Maitreya by assuming the throne of St. Peter in Rome as he *reforms* and *transforms* the Christian church "to respond correctly" to Maitreya. So this "Master Jesus"—who the Bible describes as "another Jesus" (2 Corinthians 11:4)—will be the designated "Master" who is in charge of the New Reformation of the Christian churches. Benjamin Creme wrote:

> The Master Jesus is going to reform the Christian churches.[12]

> He is one of the Masters Who will very shortly return to outer work in the world, taking over the Throne of St. Peter, in Rome. He will seek to transform the Christian Churches, in so far as they are flexible enough to respond correctly to the new reality which the return of the Christ and the Masters will create.[13]

Note: As previously mentioned, Eugene Peterson's *Message* paraphrase of the Bible often drops the words "Lord" and "Christ" from Jesus' name and title and substitutes them with the word "Master." Thus, in many *Message* verses the Lord Jesus Christ becomes only the "Master Jesus." This obviously plays right into the hands of a false Christ like Maitreya who will be trying to convince the world—and Christians alive at that time—that Jesus is not the Christ but simply the "Master Jesus" who is a disciple of "the Christ"—Maitreya.

In a New World Religion, where properly translated Christian Bibles will most likely be outlawed as "hate" literature, a hugely compromised "translation" like *The Message* could become the go-to "Bible" for a false Christ and his transformed and re-formed "Christian" church. It has already been pointed out how Peterson's *Message* has a number of overlapping occult/New Age references that play right into the hands of the coming false Christ—whoever that might be—and his proposed New World Religion.[14]

Maitreya: A Purpose-Driven False Christ

It is worth noting that a number of Maitreya's concepts and teachings also overlap with some of the teachings and resources of Purpose-Driven pastor Rick Warren—terms like *purpose, new reformation, God's Dream, God "in" everything,* and *Peace Plan* among others. In fact, these areas of overlap are already blurring some of the crucial differences between biblical Christianity and the ever-invasive teachings of the New Age/New Spirituality. Curiously, instead of warning about a false Christ figure like Maitreya, much of Rick Warren's language is sounding very similar to Maitreya. The most obvious example being that both Maitreya and Rick Warren base their teachings upon the foundational word "purpose." Long before Rick Warren's mega best-selling books *The Purpose-Driven Church* and *The Purpose-Driven Life,* Maitreya introduced the importance of purpose and of a purpose driven life. Maitreya stated:

> I need all those who long to serve, who wish to fulfil their purpose in life.[15]

> Take My hand, My friends, and let us together walk that Path and know the meaning of Life, know the blessing of Love, know the purpose of God.[16]

> I am your Purpose.[17]

> We are together, you and I, for the same purpose.[18]

> I shall place before you all the purpose of God.[19]

> Hold fast to My Purpose, which is to take man to God.[20]

> My Purpose unfolds.[21]

> My Purposes are being fulfilled.[22]

Purpose is obviously at the heart of everything Maitreya proposes. Occupying the whole back cover of the channeled book *Messages from Maitreya* is a proposed "Great Invocation" that calls for the return of Christ. This "Great Invocation" is recited in many churches around the world. "The Great Invocation"—first delivered through New Age Matriarch Alice A. Bailey in 1945—was said by Benjamin Creme to be inspired by Maitreya himself.[23] "The Great Invocation" centers on the word "purpose" as it calls for the return of "the Christ" and the implementation of his New Age "plan" for the world. The very heart of this New Age invocation is found in a key line on the back cover that invokes purpose to "guide"—to drive—our lives:

> From the centre where the Will of God is known Let purpose guide the little wills of men—The purpose which the Masters know and serve.

Several years ago, a South African pastor e-mailed me his new book that was completely devoted to exposing the parallels between *The Purpose-Driven Life* and "The Great Invocation."[24] Titled *Ultimate Deception,* the author's research confirmed and further added to the New Age implications I had observed when first reading *The Purpose-Driven Life*. My 2004 book *Deceived on Purpose: The New Age Implications of the Purpose-Driven Church* documented my findings and even had a whole chapter on Maitreya titled "False Christ with a Purpose." The chapter described some of the parallels between Rick Warren's book *The Purpose-Driven Life* with the New Age and Maitreya. Now here was this South African pastor pointing out the New Age parallels between Rick Warren's *The Purpose-Driven Life* and "The Great Invocation," reputedly inspired by Maitreya.

Maitreya's Four-fold Purpose

Maitreya appears to have at least a four-fold purpose and function: 1) Establish a New Age/New World Religion by helping humanity to fulfill God's Dream and to experience their Oneness with God and each other; 2) Bring peace to the world through his reappearance and return; 3) Introduce and help further radically progressive economic, environmental, political, spiritual, and humanitarian projects around the world; 4) Ultimately lead mankind to the feet of Sanat Kumara—who is described as "Father," "God," and "the Lord of the World."[25]

The Bible warns about Satan—"the god of this world"—who blinds the minds of those who "believe not" the truth (2 Corinthians 4:4). Maitreya, in referring to Sanat Kumara as "the Lord of the World," openly mocks this biblical passage. Sanat is actually a hidden in plain sight anagram of Satan—"the god of this world." Whether Maitreya is the Antichrist, a prototype for Antichrist, or just another false New Age Christ, the church needs to keep a definite eye on him and his New Age organization, Share International.

Immanence: The Occult/New Age "God" Within

Years ago, after reading Rick Warren's book *The Purpose-Driven Life,* I found myself looking at Maitreya in a much different light. There was something particularly disturbing about the similarity of Maitreya's and Rick Warren's immanent, God "in" everything teachings.

On page 88 in *Messages from Maitreya the Christ,* Maitreya states:

> My friends, God is nearer to you than you can imagine.
> God is yourself. God is within you and all around you.

On page 88 of *The Purpose-Driven Life,* Rick Warren says essentially the same thing. He writes:

> Because God is with you all the time, no place is any closer to God than the place where you are right now. The Bible says, "He rules everything and is everywhere and is in everything."

I also noticed how Rick Warren and Maitreya were both presenting the same foundational New Age God "in" everything teaching of immanence. On page 88 of *The Reappearance of the Christ and the Masters of Wisdom,* Benjamin Creme describes Maitreya's New World Religion. Creme writes:

> But eventually a new world religion will be inaugurated which will be a fusion and synthesis of the approach of the East and the approach of the West. The Christ will bring together, not simply Christianity and Buddhism, but the concept of God transcendent—outside of His creation—and also the concept of God immanent in all creation—in man and all creation.

Emphasizing the words "fresh," "foundational," and "immanent," renowned occult teacher and New Age matriarch Alice Bailey also described how the "foundational truths" of the New World Religion will be based on this same "immanent" New Age teaching:

> . . . a fresh orientation to divinity and to the acceptance of the fact of God Transcendent and of God Immanent within every form of life.

> These are the foundational truths upon which the world religion of the future will rest.[26]

As cited, this same foundational "immanent" aspect of God so important to Maitreya, Alice Bailey, the New Age/New Spirituality, and the New World Religion, was also important to Rick Warren. Immanence has been taught as part of the *Foundations Guide* at his Saddleback Church. Echoing Bailey's use of the words "immanence," "foundational truths," and "fresh,"[27] the *Foundations Participant's Guide: 11 Core Truths to Build Your Life On* under the section heading "A Fresh Word" reiterates Rick Warren's teaching on immanence—that God is "in" everything. It states:

> The fact that God stands above and beyond his creation does not mean he stands outside his creation. He is both transcendent (above and beyond his creation) and immanent (within and throughout his creation).[28] (Parentheses in original)

As also cited, this "immanent" New Age aspect of God shows up in Eugene Peterson's *Message*, Rick Warren's most frequently quoted Bible translation in *The Purpose-Driven Life*. This notion that God is "in" everything and is "One" with creation is found in Peterson's twisted paraphrase of the Lord's Prayer.

Counterfeit Pentecost

In *The Reappearance of the Christ and the Masters of Wisdom*, Benjamin Creme describes how Maitreya's "Day of Declaration"—his alleged "reappearance" and "return" as "the Christ"—will be celebrated throughout the world as a Second Pentecost:

> One day soon, men and women all over the world will gather round their radio and television sets to hear and see the Christ: to see His face, and to hear His words dropping silently into their minds—in their own language. In this way they will know that He is truly the Christ, the World Teacher; and in this way too, we will see repeated, only now on a world scale, the happenings of Pentecost; and in celebration of this event Pentecost will become a major festival of the New World Religion.[29]

In addressing questions about Maitreya's ability to convince skeptical Christians that he is "the Christ" and not the Antichrist, Creme described how Maitreya has been working behind the scenes with Christians for years "to soften them up."[30] He stated that on the "Day of Declaration," a powerful "Pentecostal experience for all" would convince "even the fundamentalists" that Maitreya is "the Christ." Creme wrote:

> The fundamentalists, of course, are afraid that Maitreya might be the "Antichrist," with which fallacy I have dealt many times, here and elsewhere. On the Day of Declaration, I submit, everyone—even the fundamentalists—will know, through the overshadowing of the minds of all humanity—a Pentecostal experience for all—that Maitreya is the Christ.[31]

Holy Laughter or Strong Delusion

In a 1994 article titled, "Holy Laughter or Strong Delusion?,"[32] I expressed deep concern about the "holy laughter" movement that had suddenly erupted at the Toronto Airport Vineyard church in Canada. The movement was inspired by South African evangelist Rodney Howard-Browne who was described by many of his followers as the "Holy Ghost bartender." The Toronto Blessing—as it was being called—was carried to countless other churches around the world. Congregations participating in this movement found themselves breaking into uncontrollable fits of laughter as they often fell to the ground—sometimes barking like dogs, roaring like lions, and even oinking like pigs.

Unbelievably, this "holy laughter" phenomenon was being described in many church circles as a "great move of God" and as the sign of a "great revival." It was featured positively in the Christian media and by countless pastors, churches, and Christian leaders. This strange behavior was being euphorically described by participants as the "joy of the Lord" and being "drunk in the spirit." Convinced that "holy laughter" was part of a great revival sent from God, most of the enthusiasts never thought to search the Scriptures and to pray and seek God's counsel regarding holy laughter's legitimacy (James 1:5)—to "try [test] the spirits" to see if holy laughter was really from God (1 John 4:1). Rather, the movement had more of a "go-with-the-flow" attitude, not wanting to question "what God *might* be doing."

In my article I mentioned how the late New Age leader Barbara Marx Hubbard, claiming to be in contact with "Christ," had written about a future "Planetary Pentecost" when humanity would collectively experience what was described to her as "the joy of the force." This New Age Christ, deceptively alluding to the Book of Joel, told Hubbard that a Planetary Smile would light up the face of mankind as "the joy of the force" would produce a universal experience of "uncontrollable joy." She wrote:

> The Planetary Smile is another name for the Planetary Pentecost. When enough of us share a common thought of our oneness with God, Spirit will be poured out on all flesh paying attention.[33]

> An uncontrollable joy will ripple through the thinking layer of Earth. . . . From within, all sensitive persons will feel the joy of the force, flooding their systems with love and attraction.[34]

It seems rather obvious that the New Age "Pentecostal experience for all," this "overshadowing of the minds of all humanity" with the "joy of the force," sounds a whole lot like the "holy laughter" phenomenon. Thus, the question necessarily arises—Is holy laughter part of the New Age plan to "soften up," deceive, and lead astray unsuspecting Christians? Are today's holy laughter type "revivals" simply dress rehearsals for a future Planetary Pentecost that will help to usher in the Antichrist? Perhaps the answer comes directly from the false "Jesus" who channeled the New Age "Bible"—*A Course in Miracles*. Directly refuting the true Jesus Christ's sober and prophetic warnings about the time of the end, this New Age "Jesus" states that "the world will end in laughter."[35]

Discerning False Christs

> Study to shew thyself approved unto God, a workman that needeth not to be ashamed, rightly dividing the word of truth. (2 Timothy 2:15)

Given Maitreya's alleged presence on Earth, we already know he is a false Christ because the Bible teaches that the true Christ will return from the heavens above—not from the Earth below. We are specifically told He will come in the clouds where every eye will see Him:

> For our conversation is in heaven; from whence also we look for the Saviour, the Lord Jesus Christ. (Philippians 3:20)

> Behold, he cometh with clouds; and every eye shall see him. (Revelation 1:7)

The true Christ—Jesus Christ—warns us to beware of false Christs who emerge from their earthly habitations to declare their presence in the world and in people's hearts:

> For there shall arise false Christs, and false prophets, and shall show great signs and wonders; insomuch that, if it were possible, they shall deceive the very elect. Behold, I have told you before. Wherefore if they shall say unto you, Behold, he is in the desert; go not forth: behold, he is in the secret chambers; believe it not. For as the lightning cometh out of the east, and

shineth even unto the west; so shall also the coming of the Son of man be. (Matthew 24:24-27)

The Bible is clear that the name of our true Lord and Savior is Jesus Christ—not Maitreya the Christ or anyone else the Christ.

Wherefore God also hath highly exalted him, and given him a name which is above every name: That at the name of Jesus every knee should bow, of things in heaven, and things in earth, and things under the earth; And that every tongue should confess that Jesus Christ is Lord, to the glory of God the Father. (Philippians 2:9-11)

Behold, they shall surely gather
together, but not by me: whosoever
shall gather together against thee
shall fall for thy sake. (Isaiah 54:15)

Global Revival or Global Deception? 10 Critical Warnings

Lessons From the Titanic to the Church

Who doesn't want true revival—one filled with godly sorrow, heartfelt repentance, and powerfully met with God's forgiveness, mercy, and amazing grace? But the word *true* is key. The revival must not be unduly influenced by our spiritual Adversary for his own deceptive purposes. True revival has to be truly God-given and truly inspired by our One True God and His One True Holy Spirit.

Prior to its sinking, the *RMS Titanic* was thought to be "invincible" and "unsinkable" and was viewed with widespread confidence and positive regard. People felt they would be safe on that big and mighty ship. *What could possibly go wrong?* Today, revival is seen in much the same way. It brings up similar notions of invincibility, "unsinkability," and positive regard. People feel safe when they are part of a big and mighty revival. *What could possibly go wrong?* And it is in this light that the *Titanic* can serve as a graphic example for the church today.

The following are ten critical warnings from the *Titanic* as the church longs for revival yet moves into some very dangerous waters:

I. A Little Leaven/The "God Within"

The Titanic: After the *Titanic* sank, it was generally believed that the iceberg had sliced a 300-foot-long gash piercing the ship's hull. However, a decade after the *Titanic* was finally located in 1985, a scientific expedition found out what really happened. The title of an April 8, 1997 *New York Times* article read—"Toppling Theories, Scientists Find 6 Slits, Not Big Gash, Sank *Titanic*." The account that followed revealed that the shipwreck was *not* the result of a 300-foot-long gash as previously theorized. Rather, it described how an international team of scientists discovered the damaged area to be no more than "12-13 square feet." Proving that a little leaven can leaven the entire lump, it was concluded that it only took "a series of six thin openings" totaling less than the size of "two sidewalk squares" to sink the *Titanic* in less than three hours.[1]

At the time of its sailing, it was almost inconceivable that the "unsinkable" *Titanic* could be shipwrecked at all, much less by an area no larger than "two sidewalk squares." Thus, history now records that it only took a little leaven to sink the biggest, grandest ship of its time. In similar fashion, it will only take a little leaven—like the false teaching that God is "in" everything—"God within"—to sink what may turn out to be the biggest, grandest revival of its time.

The Church: *Titanic* author and researcher Walter Lord wrote the following in his book *The Night Lives On*:

> Just 20 minutes short of midnight, April 14, 1912, the great new White Star Liner *Titanic,* making her maiden voyage from Southampton to New York, had a rendezvous with ice in the calm, dark waters of the North Atlantic.

She brushed the berg so gently that many on board didn't notice it, but so lethally that she was instantly doomed.[2]

And so it is with today's church. It has brushed up against the New Age/New Gospel teaching of the "God within" so *gently* that most people haven't noticed but so *lethally* that it could ultimately shipwreck the faith of those who do not recognize it, renounce it, and flee from it.

Ye did run well; who did hinder you that ye should not obey the truth? This persuasion cometh not of him that calleth you. A little leaven leaveneth the whole lump. (Galatians 5:7-9)

11. Ship of Dreams/God's Dream

The Titanic: Described as the "Ship of Dreams," the *RMS Titanic* was owned by the British White Star Line and was built by the Harland and Wolff shipyards in Belfast, Ireland. In almost every conceivable way, the *Titanic* seemed to be a literal "Ship of Dreams." The biggest ship and the biggest moving object of its time, the *Titanic* was a dream come true for transatlantic travelers. But in the end, the big ship and the big dream became a big nightmare. The luxurious and seemingly "unsinkable" vessel was shipwrecked five days out on its maiden voyage. Today, over a century later, the *Titanic* lies buried in its watery grave 400 miles off the coast of Newfoundland. And buried at sea with the "Ship of Dreams" were the shattered dreams of over fifteen hundred men, women, and children.

The Church: In 2003, mega-church pastor Rick Warren proclaimed that he had a big dream and a big "Peace Plan" for his big Purpose Driven movement. He called his big dream and his big plan for a big revival "God's Dream for You—and the World."[3] However, most people in today's church don't know that "God's Dream" is an overlapping New

Age term with century-old roots in Theosophy and the occult.[4] Decades later this New Age concept of "God's Dream" was picked up and popularized in the church by pastors Robert Schuller and Rick Warren. Because of them, the term "God's Dream" has become a go-to term in today's church and is commonly used by countless pastors, leaders, and everyday believers. In fact, thanks to Rick Warren and his Global Peace Plan, this overlapping New Age concept of "God's Dream" has come to symbolize world peace and world revival as it *seems* to idealize the hopes and dreams of both the world and today's church.

These two metaphors—"Ship of Dreams" and "God's Dream"—imply a powerful sense of hopeful expectation, promise, and success. Given the lofty grandeur of these two terms, how could anything possibly go wrong? Wouldn't a "Ship of Dreams" always reach its destination? Wouldn't "God's Dream" always come true? But history records what happened to the "Ship of Dreams," and the Bible warns *not so fast* with an overlapping New Age concept like "God's Dream." Scripture makes it clear that God does not dream, daydream, or pipe dream—especially when it comes to the future. God already knows the future and what it holds. Thankfully, He has warned us about it ahead of time in Scripture. Instead of a coming worldwide revival, He has warned us about an ultimate worldwide deception. And He has specifically warned us to beware of "filthy dreamers" (Jude 1:8) and dreamers of dreams who prophesy "false dreams"—like "God's Dream"—that test our faith to see if we love the Lord with all of our heart and soul (Deuteronomy 13:1-13).

> Behold, I am against them that prophesy false dreams, saith the LORD, and do tell them, and cause my people to err by their lies, and by their lightness; yet I sent them not, nor commanded them: therefore they shall not profit this people at all, saith the LORD. (Jeremiah 23:32)

III. The Launch

The Titanic: On May 31, 1911, over 100,000 people, including ninety newspaper representatives from around the world, gathered at Belfast, Ireland's Harland and Wolff shipyard and along the banks of the River Lagan to watch the public launch of the RMS *Titanic*. Amidst all the positive fanfare, who in attendance would have ever imagined they were witnessing the launch of a future disaster? And so it was with the celebrated launch of an alleged revival some eighty-two years later in Toronto, Canada. Massive numbers of people would converge on the Toronto Airport Vineyard church. They believed that the so-called "Toronto Blessing" was the launch of a great modern-day revival. And like those at the *Titanic* launch, almost no one present considered the possibility that what they were witnessing and experiencing could be the launch of a future disaster.

The Church: On January 20, 1994, the "Toronto Blessing"—an alleged outpouring of the Holy Spirit—was launched when pastor Randy Clark spoke at John Arnott's Toronto Airport Vineyard in Toronto, Canada. Clark testified that his life had been powerfully transformed by a strange new phenomenon called "holy laughter." As he spoke, people started laughing uncontrollably and falling to the floor. It was believed by most of those gathered, that through this "holy laughter," God was bringing a much needed "joy" and "revival" to His church. Within five years, over two million people had traveled to Toronto to experience what was happening. In a February 1995 article in *Toronto Life* magazine, Canadian journalist Robert Hough provided readers with some of what he witnessed regarding the "holy laughter." He wrote:

> The man sitting beside me, Dwayne from California, roared like a wounded lion. The woman beside Dwayne started jerking so badly her hands struck her face. People fell like dominoes, collapsing chairs as they plunged to the carpeting. They howled like wolves, brayed like donkeys

and—in the case of a young man standing near the sound board—started clucking like a feral chicken.[5]

Holy Ghost Bartender

The "Toronto Blessing" is now commonly regarded as the "mother ship" for many of the other "revivals" that have occurred since. Many present-day ministries, like that of Bethel's Bill Johnson, can be traced back to Toronto and the influence of a transplanted South African evangelist named Rodney Howard-Browne. He was the one who passed his "holy laughter" "anointing" on to Randy Clark and—directly or indirectly—to millions of others. However, the hysterical laughter, loss of self-control, mental confusion, and tumbling to the floor—sometimes for hours—bore no resemblance to past *true* revivals. In those revivals, godly sorrow and deep repentance were characteristic—not ungodly manifestations like "holy laughter" (2 Corinthians 7:10).

No Laughing Matter

In spite of the controversy that surrounded it, the "Toronto Blessing" convinced many church leaders that God was in the process of unleashing an "international awakening"—a great worldwide revival. Veteran church figure Michael Brown wrote a book titled *From Holy Laughter to Holy Fire: America on the Edge of Revival.* He believed that the "Toronto Blessing" was the launch of an "international awakening" of "huge" proportions.[6] Toronto pastor John Arnott said the church needed to prepare for "the greatest harvest of souls the world has ever seen."[7] Church leader and present-day revivalist Leonard Sweet stated that God was in the process of giving "birth" to the "greatest spiritual awakening" in "the history of the church."[8] Across the board, church figures from Pat Robertson, Kenneth Copeland, Beth Moore, and Rick Warren to Greg Laurie, Jonathan Roumie, Dutch Sheets, and William Paul Young are all heralding a mighty move of God—a great worldwide revival. But none of them seem to be concerned that the false New Age Christ and his designated false teachers have been heralding the very same thing.

New Age Planetary Pentecost

Thus, what is being seriously overlooked by today's church is that the false New Age/New Gospel Christ describes *his* worldwide revival as a "Planetary Pentecost."[9] Today's church leaders, using much the same language, describe their worldwide revival as a "Second Pentecost."[10] And there seems to be no awareness—much less concern by today's church leadership—of how these two parallel revivals could eventually merge in the future and become dangerously "One."

Sounding just like "holy laughter," the New Age Christ states that in his Planetary Pentecost, people will experience "the joy of the force flooding their systems with love and attraction."[11] He says this "joy of the force" will produce "a Pentecostal experience for all"—"even the fundamentalists."[12] He says that his Planetary Pentecost—his world revival—will bring peace and healing to the world and that "the world will end in laughter."[13]

IV. Misplaced Confidence in Technology

The Titanic: Prior to the disaster, the *Irish News and Belfast Morning News* headlined the *Titanic* as "A Masterpiece of Irish Brains and Industry."[14] Until its demise, the *Titanic* was a supreme symbol of the Gilded Age notion that man and his "smart" technology had finally outsmarted the forces of nature. Grand possibility thinking seemed to prevail throughout the land. With the rapid advances being made in technology, even the impossible seemed possible. The *Titanic,* with all of its sheer opulence, bold bigness, and technological superiority, stood as proof positive that man could not only dream the impossible dream, he could now make that dream come true. As far as the world was concerned, the *Titanic* was—in every conceivable way—a "Ship of Dreams." However, at the height of this seemingly invincible era of big money, big business, big buildings, big ships, and big dreams—the big dream went under. So much for the *Titanic's* state-of-the-art "smart" technology. The "unsinkable" ship was gone, and so was the dream. The triumph of modern technology and the unbridled dreams of the Gilded Age had suddenly hit the wall.

Similarly, certain physicists and self-described "futurists"—both in the New Age and in today's church—have manipulated legitimate discoveries in quantum physics to produce what appears to be a seemingly scientific technologically based *quantum spirituality.* This New Age/New Spirituality promises to bring an otherwise divided world into harmonic convergence and spiritual Oneness. Proponents of this quantum spirituality believe it will unify the world and all its various religions. In fact, the world and the church are being told that a New Age/New World Religion is now possible because quantum technology is allegedly proving that God is "in" everyone and everything.

The Church: One of the most deceptive "Christian" books in this quantum area is Leonard Sweet's *Quantum Spirituality: A Postmodern Apologetic.* In his 1991 book, Sweet actually praises a number of New Age leaders for being his "personal role models" and "heroes."[15] He even credits them for helping him to develop his "quantum spirituality," which redefines, reinterprets, and ultimately reinvents biblical Christianity in quantum God "in" everything New Age terms.

In his mega best-selling 1975 book, *The Tao of Physics: An Exploration of the Parallels Between Modern Physics and Eastern Mysticism,* New Age physicist Fritjov Capra stated that "our own spiritual traditions will have to undergo some radical changes in order to be in harmony with the values of the new paradigm."[16] Sixteen years later in *Quantum Spirituality,* Leonard Sweet proposed just such a "radical" change. Agreeing with New Age quantum advocates like Fritjov Capra, Sweet introduced the "radical doctrine" of the "God within"—the "God" who is "in" everyone and everything—as the spiritual foundation for his quantum spirituality. He stated:

> Quantum spirituality bonds us to all creation as well as to other members of the human family. . . . This entails a radical doctrine of embodiment of God in the very substance of creation.[17]

In 1912, as the *Titanic* departed from Southampton, England, this "unsinkable" "smart" ship was proclaimed to be an incredibly advanced state-of-the-art technological wonder. Five days later all that "smart" technology lay shipwrecked at the bottom of the Atlantic Ocean. Likewise, today's wayward world and wayward church, with all its "smart" quantum technology and its "smart" quantum spirituality is, like the *Titanic*, just another disaster waiting to happen. It bears repeating that the apostle Paul warned Timothy—and all of us—to beware of anything that presents itself as being scientifically and technologically superior when, in reality, it is not:

> O Timothy, keep that which is committed to thy trust, avoiding profane and vain babblings, and oppositions of science falsely so called: Which some professing have erred concerning the faith. (1 Timothy 6:20-21)

V. Wasted Warnings

The Titanic: The April presence of icebergs and ice fields in North Atlantic waters was no surprise to Captain Edward Smith and his *Titanic* officers. Iceberg awareness was an important part of their job and training. So what happened? When Captain Smith and his crew set out in April, they were aware that ice could be a problem. In the warm spring of 1912, the Labrador current had brought especially large ice-flows down from Greenland and into the North Atlantic shipping lanes where many ocean liners traveled. In addition to this knowledge, the *Titanic* received six specific warnings en route about the dangerous ice fields that lay before them. Not what *might* lie ahead of them, but what *did* lie ahead of them. Yet, in spite of these warnings, Captain Smith had the ship sailing at nearly full speed as he neared the treacherous iceberg on that fatal April night. In the end, the six warning messages that were lightly regarded, ignored, or just plain missed by the *Titanic* officers, played a huge role in the *Titanic* shipwreck. And so it is with today's church.

The Church: Serious warnings have been issued throughout the years describing how the New Age/New Gospel deception has been seeping into the church. However, these warnings often have come from outside of established church leadership circles. And like the warnings to the *Titanic*, these warnings have been lightly regarded, ignored, or just plain missed by most church leaders. Thus, despite the warnings—including from those who actually came out of the New Age and the occult—today's church appears to be sailing full speed ahead into a revival that is fraught with danger and the very real potential for spiritual disaster.

> Wherefore let him that thinketh he standeth take heed lest he fall. (1 Corinthians 10:12)

VI. Racing Toward Disaster

The Titanic: The United States Senate Subcommittee Hearing on the *Titanic* began on April 19, 1912, just four days after the disaster. After everyone had spoken, and all the evidence weighed, the subcommittee unanimously concluded that one of the chief factors causing the disaster was the ship's excessive speed—especially when they had been repeatedly warned of the dangerous ice fields that lay before them.[18] Twelve days after the disaster, an April 27, 1912 article in *Scientific American* directly attributed the shipwreck to Captain Smith's "high speed" at night in the midst of heavy ice fields.[19]

The night of the disaster, Mrs. Charlotte Collyer recalled a ship stewardess telling her that they were heading into a "dangerous part of the ocean" known as the "Devil's Hole." Rather than being frightened, Mrs. Collyer said she remained undismayed. She believed the crew was aware of the danger and would be taking all the proper precautions to ensure their safety. Feeling calm and safe, Mrs. Collyer fell asleep in her cozy cabin. However, in a few short hours she would be shivering in a lifeboat, watching the ship where she had felt so safe, sink right in front of her.[20]

The Church: Charlotte Collyer trusted that everything was alright because she believed the *Titanic* officers were looking out for everyone. She was not aware that they were not taking the necessary precautions to insure everyone's safety and physical well-being. Similarly, most of today's church assumes that its leaders are looking out for their safety and spiritual well-being. However, like Captain Smith and his officers racing their "ship of dreams" into a total disaster, today's church leaders are racing their "God's Dream" church into a world revival that has all the makings of a similar disaster.

As cited, church revivalist and New Age sympathizer, Leonard Sweet, states that the church is in "a race to the future." He says in the name of "God's Dream," God is giving "birth" to the "greatest spiritual awakening" in "the history of the church." Bethel Church senior pastor Bill Johnson similarly states—"We are in a race. It's a race between what is and what could be."[21] But the Bible makes it clear that we are not in a race to fulfill an overlapping New Age concept like "God's Dream." And we are not in a race to have the greatest revival in history. Rather, the race is for those who take time to heed the warnings they have been given. The race is for those who understand that deception can come in almost any form—even in the form of a worldwide revival. In short, the race is for those who know "the race is not to the swift" (Ecclesiastes 9:11) but for those who "run with patience the race that is set before us."

> Wherefore seeing we also are compassed about with so great a cloud of witnesses, let us lay aside every weight, and the sin which doth so easily beset us, and let us run with patience the race that is set before us. (Hebrews 12:1)

VII. Taking Things Too Lightly

The Titanic: After the *Titanic* collided with the iceberg, and with water flooding into the bowels of the vessel, some of the passengers frolicked in an almost party-like atmosphere around the two tons of ice that had spilled out onto the foredeck of the already sinking ship. Several hours later, some of those involved in the merry making would be fighting for their lives in the freezing Atlantic Ocean.

After the collision with the ice, young Jack Thayer told his parents that he was "going out to see the fun."[22] Mrs. Natalie Wick noticed that passengers were picking up pieces of the ice and "playfully throwing chunks at each other."[23] Major Arthur Godfrey Peuchen reported meeting a friend on the stairway who "laughingly" told him that they had struck an iceberg.[24] Lawrence Beesley recalled how "snowballing matches" were already planned for the next morning.[25]

The Church: So it is with an undiscerning church that delights itself in the "holy laughter" that often accompanies modern-day "revivals" like the "Toronto Blessing." The party-like atmosphere of these "revivals" is reminiscent of *Titanic* passengers, who, unaware of the disaster unfolding around them, wanted to be part of "the fun." *Charisma* magazine, reporting on the "Toronto Blessing" in August 1994, wrote about those who went to Toronto to "join the fun."[26] In describing the "Toronto Blessing," pastor Randy Clark said that sometimes there was "so much laughter" going on in the services that it seemed to be "more of a party than church"[27] He recounted how one man said—"It's like someone's throwing one big party."[28] In *The Secret Message of Jesus*, emergent church figure Brian McLaren wrote how God is inviting everyone to "a party."[29]

Jesus Is a Party Person?

Rick Warren sent a January 29, 2020 e-mail to his church. It was framed with the heading "Time to Dream" and titled "The Power and Purpose of Parties." He used his e-mail to present what he called a "mini-Bible study" on "The Power and Purpose of Parties." He said that Jesus was so into partying that today's pharisees would call Jesus "a party animal."[30] Rick Warren's effort to present Jesus as a big "party" person seemed more than a little strange. But not to Rodney Howard-Browne, Randy Clark, Brian McLaren, and all the other church leaders who also portray Jesus as a last days "party" person.

Given these comments and given the state of the world today, is all this "partying" in the name of Jesus and the Holy Spirit in any way realistic? Are future revivals going to be spiritual offshoots of the "Toronto Blessing"—"like someone's throwing one big party?" Are we to believe that the "someone" throwing the "big party" is going to be Jesus Himself because he is "so into partying?" Was the "Toronto Blessing" a dress rehearsal for future "revivals" that will ultimately usher in a false New Age Christ who is already on record saying that "the world will end in laughter?" And are we really supposed to believe the true Jesus told Sarah Young and her millions of *Jesus Calling* readers to "laugh at the future?"[31]

For those who have a love of the truth and a love of the true Jesus Christ, we are told to work out our salvation with "fear and trembling." We are not told to work out our salvation with "holy laughter"-type partying. We are not to take part in "revivals" that have "another Jesus"—a "party Jesus"—who is not the true Jesus Christ. We are not to take part in "revivals" that have "another spirit"—a "party spirit"—that may one day merge with the false New Age Christ's "joy of the force" and his Planetary Pentecost.

> For if he that cometh preacheth another Jesus, whom we have not preached, or if ye receive another spirit, which ye have not received, or another gospel, which ye have not accepted, ye might well bear with him. (2 Corinthians 11:4)

VIII. Sacrificing Safety for Greed and Gain

The Titanic: It is a tragic fact that there were not enough lifeboats for all the *Titanic* passengers and crew. As a result, more than 1500 people unnecessarily died. One of the chief reasons for the shortage was because archaic shipping regulations didn't require shipping lines to have a sufficient number of lifeboats for everyone on board. And because the White Star Line didn't have to have them—they didn't. The ship owners knew that by cutting back on lifeboats, they could cut their costs. And with fewer lifeboats, there would be additional deck space to make the ship more attractive and comfortable for potential ticket buyers. In short, maximizing the company's financial gain took precedence over maximizing the safety of their passengers.

The Church: This same emphasis on financial gain has always been present in certain segments of the professing church. From overly solicitous prosperity preachers to spiritually compromised books like *The Shack* and *Jesus Calling,* undiscerning and unsuspecting believers are often unaware of how they are being used and manipulated for both commercial and spiritual purposes.

As cited before, in 2013, people started to become aware that *God Calling,* the book that inspired Sarah Young to do *Jesus Calling,* was actually a channeled New Age book.[32] As a result, Young and her publishers did some quick damage control to preserve the popularity and profitability of their mega best-selling book. Realizing that *Jesus Calling* was suddenly being regarded as a channeled New Age book, Young and her editors removed all references to *God Calling* from all subsequent printings of her book. They also removed the sections where Young stated that her daily devotions were direct messages from Jesus Himself—including many that had New Age implications and others that stretched or contradicted Scripture. They even changed her mystical moonlight conversion to a more acceptable and traditional conversion account. But there was no explanation for these changes.[33] Future readers would never know about the damage control Young and her editors had done to try and salvage the credibility of their book.

Thus, just as the *Titanic* owners had sacrificed the *physical safety* of their trusting passengers for profit and gain, Young and her editors sacrificed the *spiritual safety* of their trusting readers for profit and gain. The Bible describes what Young and the *Titanic* owners did as the merchandising of men's souls:

> The merchandise of gold, and silver, and precious stones, and of pearls, and fine linen, and purple, and silk, and scarlet . . . and souls of men. (Revelation 18:12-13)

IX. Church Revival Leaders Talking With the Dead?

The Titanic: William T. Stead (1849-1912) was a renowned British journalist, professing Christian and practicing spiritualist, who was famously known for his investigative articles, books, social activism, and revival advocacy. As a *Titanic* passenger, he was on his way to speak at a World Peace Conference in New York City at the request of American President William Howard Taft. Stead was one of the over 1500 people who perished at sea.

As a professing "Christian," Stead was also deeply involved in "spiritualism"—what would be referred to today as New Age spirituality. He claimed to have a spiritual gift that enabled the spirit of another person to communicate through his passive writing hand in an occult practice known as automatic writing. In publishing the numerous "letters" that were allegedly written through him by a deceased friend named Julia Ames, he hoped to normalize the occult practice of communicating with the dead. In particular, he wanted to share the spiritual counsel he had received from "Julia" with the world at large. For example, in a meeting "Julia" said she had with "Jesus," he told her he was going to teach her about "the secret things of God."[34] And one of the things he taught her was the "secret" of the "God within." Writing through Stead, she said that "Jesus" told her, "The object of life is to evoke, to develop the God within."[35] This "secret" of the "God within" was revealed in Stead's book, *After Death: Letters From Julia* (1905) and was described under the bold heading—"A Spiritual Revival."

"Spiritual Revival"

Through Stead, "Julia" wrote that a worldwide revival—"a great spiritual awakening among the nations"—would take place in the future as humanity "awakened" to "the immanence of the Divine"—the "God within"—that was universally "in" themselves and "in" their fellow man. "Julia" said:

> I was at first astonished to learn how much importance the spirits attach to the communications which they are allowed to have with those on earth. I can, of course, easily understand, because I feel it myself—the craving there is to speak to those whom you loved . . . but it is much more than this. What they tell me on all sides, and especially my dear guides, is that the time is come when there is to be a great spiritual awakening among the nations, and that the agency which is to bring this about is the sudden and conclusive demonstration, in every individual case which seeks for it, of the reality of the spirit, of the permanence of the soul, and the immanence of the Divine.[36]

And what "Julia" was taught by "Jesus" and her "guides" over a century ago about "the immanence of the Divine" and "a great spiritual awakening among the nations," is exactly what is being taught by both New Age leaders and church leaders today: that this "great spiritual awakening" is approaching. But again, the Bible makes no mention of a great worldwide revival at the end of time. To the contrary, it warns of a great worldwide deception replete with false signs and wonders (Revelation 18:23, Matthew 24:24).

Surprisingly, William Stead, as a hybridized New Age "Christian," was greatly involved in the Welsh Revival. His 1905 book, *The Welsh Revival of 1904-1905*, promoted the revival and sold over 700,000 copies in Britain and America combined.[37] Four years later, he released another book titled *How I Know the Dead Return*. It was a personal account of his alleged communication with his deceased son William. A century later, a Tennessee pastor and his wife also wrote a book about their alleged communication with their deceased son—only his name was Josiah.

The Church: In 2010, Steve Berger, who was head pastor of the Grace Chapel mega-church in Leiper's Fork, Tennessee, co-wrote a book with his wife Sarah titled *Have Heart: Bridging the Gulf Between Heaven and Earth*. It describes how the couple claimed to be interacting with their deceased son, Josiah. The book contains the front-cover endorsement of televangelist James Robison (*Life Today* TV host) and the front-page endorsement of pastor Greg Laurie. It also contains the endorsement of *Shack* author and self-proclaimed universalist, William Paul Young. Young was, in effect, reciprocating Berger's front-page endorsement of *The Shack,* where Berger called *The Shack* "spiritually profound" and "theologically enlightening" and wrote how he had been handing out copies of Young's book by the case.

Like William Stead's *How I Know the Dead Return, Have Heart* seems to be the Bergers' attempt to normalize the practice of interacting with the dead—particularly for Christians. Closely associated with sorcery, interaction with the dead is clearly forbidden in the Bible. It is described as necromancy and as an "abomination unto the LORD" (Deuteronomy 18:10-12).

When Steve Berger was questioned by Chris Lawson of the Spiritual Research Network about his alleged communication with his son, Berger strongly defended what he and his wife were doing. He told Lawson—"God has made an exception at this time in history for the Berger family. We are, indeed, in communication with our son Josiah."[38] When Lawson tried to contact Greg Laurie about his endorsement of *Have Heart*, Laurie's secretary told Lawson—"Greg is not available for comments on that book."[39]

The Return

On September 26, 2020, a huge, highly publicized revival event, "The Return," was held on the grounds of the National Mall in Washington D.C. The Return website stated that the organization was formed to achieve the "end-goal of world revival." Yet, speaking in a prime-time slot following The Return's co-chair Jonathan Cahn was none other than pastor Steve Berger. He said his "assignment" was to take the 250,000 people gathered at the Mall and the millions watching online and to "transition" them from "repentance" into "revival."[40] Amazingly, Berger, unrepentant about his interacting with the dead, was now a leading spokesman for repentance and world revival. In the twelve years since writing *Have Heart*, rather than being confronted and held accountable for communicating with the dead, his stature in the church has only grown. Now, as a prominent revival leader, he sits on the Promise Keepers Board of Directors and their Pastoral Advisory Board.[41] He also presides over his own ministry—Ambassador Services International—in Washington D.C., where he claims to be "influencing the influencers." He also speaks at various church conferences at the invitation of respected figures like Amir Tsarfati.[42]

The "Dead" Want to Help Us?

New Age author James Redfield followed up his mega best-selling novel *The Celestine Prophecy* with another popular novel titled *The Twelfth Insight: The Hour of Decision*. When the book's New Age seekers desperately search for secret knowledge that can save the world, Rachel, one of the story's main characters, suddenly finds herself having "a real interaction" with her deceased mother. Much like William Stead's "Julia," who stressed the great importance that spirits attach to their communications with those on Earth,[43] Rachel was told much the same thing by her mother. Rachel said:

> All we have to do is use more of our power to tune in and have a conversation. It's never too late. And there is so much *more* they want to tell us.
>
> In fact, my mother said they desperately need to speak with us, right now, at this crucial point in history. They know the real Plan for the human world, and it's time for us on this side to understand.[44]

And it was that plan that has already been conveyed by so many other "seducing spirits" from the "other side." It is the plan for humanity to universally unite by "awakening" to the "God within." It was in relation to such spiritual beliefs, the apostle Paul warned:

> Now the Spirit speaketh expressly, that in the latter times some shall depart from the faith, giving heed to seducing spirits, and doctrines of devils. (1 Timothy 4:1)

X. The Iceberg and The Antichrist

The Titanic: Soon after the *Titanic* disaster, author Thomas Hardy wrote a stark poem about the "smart ship" that was not so smart. It was titled "The Convergence of the Twain.[45] "Convergence" has been commonly defined as the Oneness that results from "two or more things coming together, joining together or evolving into one."[46] And it was this disastrous "convergence" with the iceberg—this "wedded oneness" as Hardy put it—that resulted in the *Titanic's* demise and gave title to Hardy's poem. Describing the circumstances preceding the fateful "convergence" of the ship and the iceberg, the poet wrote:

> And as the smart ship grew, in stature, grace and hue, in shadowy silent distance grew the iceberg too.

The Church: Curiously, this 1912 poem can also serve as a metaphoric harbinger for the "convergence" of the world and a deceived professing church with the ultimate spiritual iceberg—Antichrist. If Hardy were alive today, he could similarly describe how a not so "smart" church was underestimating its spiritual Adversary, just as the *Titanic* had done with the iceberg.

Pierre Teilhard de Chardin, the "Father" of the New Age movement, used this same word "convergence" to falsely allege that "the only possible conversion of the world" to "a religion of the future" would require a "general convergence" of the world's religions "upon a universal Christ."[47] He wrote:

> A general convergence of religions upon the universal Christ who fundamentally satisfies them all: that seems to me the only possible conversion of the world, and the only form in which a religion of the future can be conceived.[48]

Yet, in his book *Quantum Spirituality*, church leader Leonard Sweet would have today's church believe that Teilhard was "Twentieth-century Christianity's major voice."[49] In another Sweet book, *soulTsunami*, with its front cover endorsement by Rick Warren, Sweet states that if today's church is smart it will "build new arks"[50] and submit to the smart leadership of men like himself. Why? Because in his book *AquaChurch*, he presents what he believes to be the "essential leadership arts for piloting your church in today's fluid culture."[51] However, his modern-day "ark"—his "Ship of God's

Dreams"—bears an uncanny resemblance to that 1912 "Ship of Dreams" that ended up at the bottom of the ocean.

Tragically, Captain Smith and his *Titanic* officers did not successfully "pilot" their ship through those much warned about ice-laden waters. And contrary to Leonard Sweet's *AquaChurch* assertions, he and other church leaders are not successfully "piloting" the church through "today's fluid culture." Scripture is replete with "iceberg warnings" about the deception, betrayal, and disaster that will occur in the latter days. But today's church leaders, much like the *Titanic's* ship officers, remain all too complacent about the danger that looms before them as they race toward world revival.

Shipwrecks happen when serious warnings are not taken seriously. It only took a little leaven the size of "two sidewalk squares" to shipwreck a seemingly "unsinkable" ship like the *Titanic*. And it will only take a little leaven—the false teaching of "God within"—to shipwreck a seemingly "unsinkable" church.

The *Titanic*—the "Ship of Dreams"—was shockingly unprepared for the danger that was up ahead as it raced toward the iceberg. Similarly, today's church—the "Ship of God's Dreams"—is shockingly unprepared for the danger up ahead as it races towards "world revival."

Sadly, the trap has been set. The trigger has been pulled. Antichrist—the ultimate spiritual iceberg—is drawing closer and closer as his Planetary Pentecost and Antichrist system seek to rise from the sea and converge with a deluded world and professing church.

> And I stood upon the sand of the sea, and saw a beast rise
> up out of the sea, having seven heads and ten horns, and
> upon his horns ten crowns, and upon his heads the name
> of blasphemy. (Revelation 13:1)

Epilogue

Over the last four decades, the *unholy* spirit and deceptive false teachings of a New Age/New Gospel have worked their way into an undiscerning and all-too-gullible church. Pastors and church leaders who decades ago warned about New Age deception have hardly talked about it since. As a result, this New Gospel of the New Age is presently viewed by most believers as a long-ago past occurrence even as its overlapping terms, false teachings, and deceptive practices continue to creep into the church.

Thus, while many church leaders and pastors talk about the cultural challenges of the day and the need for revival, they say almost nothing about our Adversary's spiritual schemes and devices. And while these same leaders write dramatic books and letters exhorting the church to be "courageous," to "speak out," and to "not be silenced," they have been effectively silenced themselves when it comes to spiritual deception in the church. Instead of exposing spiritual evil, contending for the faith, and fighting the good fight, they often advocate, endorse, or turn a blind eye to the very things they should be confronting. We have church leaders who claim to preach the Gospel and urge repentance while they interact with the dead, hail New Age leaders as their "heroes," and put their own chosen words in the mouths of Jesus and His disciples.

There is a lot more going on in the church than just "wokism" and "cancel culture." There is a cancelling of the true Gospel and replacing it with a new gospel. There is a cancelling of biblical Christianity and replacing it with a New Age/New Gospel that will eventually blend right into a New World Religion. Instead of a church that is contending for and defending the faith, truth is being sacrificed on the altar of unity for the sake of so-called revival. But sacrificing truth will never bring about genuine revival. Any revival that doesn't include *true* repentance and a *true* turning away from the spiritual deception in its midst is no revival at all. Instead, it will be a Trojan Horse revival that only looks like revival on the outside but inside will be filled with false teachers, false teachings, and dead men's bones. It may appear to be spirit filled, when it is actually filled with spirits. It will be like the church of Sardis, having a reputation for being spiritually alive when, in reality, it is spiritually dead (Revelation 3:1).

Century-Old Warning

In 1898—fourteen years before the sinking of the *Titanic*—a Connecticut pastor named Samuel J. Andrews was concerned about the spiritual state of the church. In particular, he was concerned about the immanent God "in" everything leaven that was streaming into the church: how this was in the process of creating a false New Age/New Gospel/New Christianity. In fact, he used the term "new age" over and over in describing the spiritual deception.[1]

To expose the deception, he wrote a book titled *Christianity and Anti-Christianity in Their Final Conflict*. In it, he described how the Antichrist was paving the way for his "God within" New Age/New Gospel and was putting forth the prospect of a worldwide revival.

However, quoting Scripture after Scripture, Andrews said that the Bible made it clear that prior to Jesus' return, there would be *no* true worldwide revival—*no* worldwide conversion to the true Christ—only worldwide hostility towards those who were committed to the true Jesus Christ and were holding to His true teachings. Pastor Andrews wrote:

> This summary of the Lord's teaching shows us that anything like a conversion of the world before His return by

the preaching of the gospel, was not in His thoughts. Had it been, He could not have failed to comfort His mourning disciples and encourage them to vigorous action by assurances of the success of their mission. But He persistently holds up before them hatred, persecution, death. His life on earth was prophetic of the history of the Church; and the greatest manifestation of hostility to her, as to Him, would be at the end.[2]

What irony, that over a century ago, this Connecticut pastor was warning about the very New Age/New Gospel deception that is not being warned about by today's church leaders.

But thank God for those precious few leaders today, who, like Samuel Andrews, "have a love of the truth," and are concerned enough to warn the church about what is going on—and are willing to actively contend for the faith which was once delivered to the saints.

> Beloved, when I gave all diligence to write unto you of the common salvation, it was needful for me to write unto you, and exhort you that ye should earnestly contend for the faith which was once delivered unto the saints. (Jude 1:3)

Endnotes

Chapter 1: The False New Age Gospel

1. Neale Donald Walsch, *Happier Than God: Turn Ordinary Life Into an Extraordinary Experience* (Ashland, OR: Emnin Books, 2008), p. 207.

2. Neale Donald Walsch, *Tomorrow's God: Our Greatest Spiritual Challenge* (New York, NY: Atria Books, 2004), p. 167.

3. Ibid., p. 167.

4. Two Listeners, Edited by A. J. Russell, *God Calling* (Grand Rapids, MI: A Spire Book published by Jove Publications Inc., for Fleming H. Revell, 2005), p. 55.

5. Ibid., p. 88.

6. Alice A, Bailey, *The Reappearance of the Christ* (New York, NY: Lucis Publishing Company, Lucis Press, Ltd., 1948, 1996), p. 150.

7. Norman Vincent Peale, *The Power of Positive Thinking* (New York, NY, Prentice-Hall, Inc., Sixteenth Printing, 1955), p. 40.

8. Pierre Teilhard de Chardin, *Christianity and Evolution* (New York, NY, Harcourt Brace Jovanovich, Inc., 1971), p. 128.

9. Ibid., p. 56.

10. *A Course in Miracles: Combined Volume* (Glen Ellen, CA: Foundation for Inner Peace, 1975) (Text), p. 147.

11. Ibid., p. 125.

12. M. Scott Peck, *The Road Less Traveled: A New Psychology of Love, Traditional Values and Spiritual Growth* (New York, NY: Simon & Schuster, 1978), p. 281.

13. Marilyn Ferguson, *The Aquarian Conspiracy: Personal and Social Transformation in the 1970s* (Los Angeles, CA: J.P. Tarcher, Inc., 1980), p. 27.

14. Ibid., p. 382.

15. *Messages from Maitreya the Christ: One Hundred Forty Messages* (Los Angeles, CA: Share International Foundation, 1980), p. 88.

16. Benjamin Creme, *The Reappearance of the Christ and the Masters of Wisdom* (London, England; The Tara Press, 1980), p. 88.

17. Shirley MacLaine, *Out on a Limb* (New York, NY: Bantam Books, 1983), p. 317.

18. *The Oprah Winfrey Show* # W265, "The New Age Movement," Air Date: September 18, 1987.

19. David Spangler and William Irwin Thompson, *Reimagination of the World: A Critique of the New Age, Science, and Popular Culture* (Santa Fe, NM: Bear & Company Publishing, 1991), p. 148.

20. Leonard Sweet, *Quantum Spirituality: A Postmodern Apologetic* (Dayton, OH: Whaleprints for SpiritVenture Ministries, Inc., 1991, 1994), p. 125.

21. Betty J. Eadie, *Embraced by the Light* (Placerville, CA: Gold Leaf Press, 1992), p. 81.

22. Sue Monk Kidd, *The Dance of the Dissident Daughter: A Woman's Journey From Christian Tradition to the Sacred Feminine* (New York, NY: Harper Collins Publishers Inc.,1992), p. 160.

23. Ronald S. Miller and the Editors of *New Age Journal, As Above, So Below: Paths to Spiritual Renewal in Daily Life* (Los Angeles, CA: Jeremy P. Tarcher Inc., 1992), p. xi.

24. Eugene Peterson, *The Message: The New Testament in Contemporary Language* (Colorado Springs, CO: NavPress, 1993, 2003), pp. 21-22.

25. Jack Canfield and Mark Victor Hansen, *Chicken Soup for the Soul: 101 Stories to Open the Heart and Rekindle the Spirit* (Deerfield Beach, FL: Health Communications, Inc., 1993), p. 69.

26. *Catechism of the Catholic Church* (New York, NY: Doubleday, 1995), p. 228.

27. Ibid., p. 129.

28. Ibid.

29. Neale Donald Walsch, *Conversations With God: an uncommon dialogue, Book 1* (New York: NY: G.P. Putnam's Sons, Hardcover Edition, 1996), p. 202.

30. Henri Nouwen, *Here and Now* (New York, NY: The Crossroad Publishing Company, 1997 edition), p. 22.

31. Leonard Sweet, *soulTsunami: Sink or Swim in the New Millennium Culture* (Grand Rapids, Mi: Zondervan, 1999), p. 28.

32. Rick Warren, *The Purpose-Driven Life: What on Earth Am I Here For?* (Grand Rapids, MI: Zondervan, 2002), p. 88.

33. *Hour of Power*, Robert H. Schuller, Program #1762, "God's Word: Rebuild, Renew, Restore" (November 9, 2003, http://www.hourofpower.org/bookletdetail.cfm?ArticleID=2107), p. 5.

34. Tom Holliday and Kay Warren, *Foundations Participant's Guide: 11 Core Truths to Build Your Life on* (Grand Rapids, MI: Zondervan, 2003), p. 46.

35. Sarah Young, *Jesus Calling* (Nashville, TN: Thomas Nelson, 2004), p. 199.

36. Rhonda Byrne, *The Secret* (New York, NY: Atria Books, 2006), p. 164.

37. *What the Bleep Do We know!?* (20th Century Fox, 2004, http://www.whatthebleep.com), transcribed by author.

38. Elizabeth Gilbert, *Eat, Pray, Love: One Woman's Search for Everything Across Italy, India and Indonesia* (New York, NY: Penguin Books, 2006), p. 192.

39. William P. Young, *The Shack: Where Tragedy Confronts Eternity* (Newbury Park, CA: Windblown Media, 2007), p. 112.

40. Glenn Beck and Dr. Keith Ablow, *The Seven Wonders That Will Change Your Life* (New York, NY: Threshold Editions-Mercury Radio Arts, A division of Simon & Schuster, Inc., 2011), p. 58.

41. Pope Francis, "Pope Offers New Beatitudes for Saints of a New Age" (*Catholic News Service*, November 1, 2016, http://www.catholicnews.com/services/englishnews/2016/pope-offers-new-beatitudes-for-saints-of-a-new-age.cfm).

42. Matthew Fox, "What Is Creation Spirituality? (https://web.archive.org/web/20120830190144/http://www.matthewfox.org/what-is-creation-spirituality).

43. Loma Dueck interview with Roma Downey (100 Huntley Street Canadian TV, https://www.youtube.com/watch?v=q2RXVCZm01k), at the 1:50 mark.

44. Richard Rohr, *The Universal Christ: How a Forgotten Reality Can Change Everything We See, Hope for, and Believe* (New York, NY: Convergent Books, 2019), p. 33.

45. Grace Salceanu, "Finding God in All Things" (https://www.jesuits.org/stories/finding-god-in-all-things).

Chapter 2: Oneness vs. Separation Heresy

1. https://www.primevideo.com/region/na/detail/Restoring-the-Shack/0QX-2V9PCIE99XH7CLAD6UB6DQI?ref_=atv_auth_pre.

2. *Restoring the Shack* television series, Trinity Broadcasting Network (TBN), episodes that were originally broadcast in 2017. Originally at https://www.tbn.org/programs/restoring-shack, but TBN removed the archive links and now sells it in DVD format.

3. Warren B. Smith, *Be Still and Know That You Are Not God: God Is Not in Everyone and Everything* (Roseburg, OR: Lighthouse Trails Publishing, 2015).

4. Neale Donald Walsch, *Tomorrow's God: Our Greatest Spiritual Challenge*, op. cit., pp. 31-32.

5. William P. Young, *The Shack*, op. cit., p. 112.

6. *A Course in Miracles, Combined Volume*, op. cit. (Text), p. 147.

7. Ibid. (Text), p. 125.

8. *Messages From Maitreya the Christ: 140 Messages*, op. cit., p. 108.

9. Ibid., p. 104.

10. *A Course in Miracles, Combined Volume*, op. cit. (Text), p. 50.

11. Neale Donald Walsch, *Conversations With God: Book 3* (Charlottesville, VA: Hampton Roads Publishing Company, Inc., 1998), p. 56.

12. Barbara Marx Hubbard, *The Revelation: A Message of Hope for the New Millennium* (Novato, CA: Nataraj Publishing, 1995), p. 193.

13. *Restoring the Shack* television series, Trinity Broadcasting Network (TBN), episode 5, March 12, 2017. Beaver dam discourse starts around the 19 minute mark. Transcribed by author.

14. *A Course in Miracles, Combined Volume*, op. cit. (Text), p. 14.

15. Neale Donald Walsch, *Conversations With God: Book 2* (Charlottesville, VA: Hampton Roads Publishing Company, Inc., 1997), p. 173.

16. Neale Donald Walsch, *Friendship With God: An Uncommon Dialogue* (New York, NY: G. P. Putnam's Sons, 1999), p. 21.

17. *A Course in Miracles, Combined Volume*, op. cit. (Manual), p. 56.

18. C. Baxter Kruger, *The Shack Revisited: There Is More Going on Here Than You Ever Dared to Dream* (New York, NY: Faith Words, 2012), p. ix.

19. C. Baxter Kruger, *Patmos, Three Days, Two Men, One Extraordinary Conversation* (Jackson, MS: Perichoresis Press, 2016), p. 90.

20. Ibid., p. 91.

21. Ibid.

22. Ibid., p. 93.

23. Ibid., p. 92.

24. Ibid., p. 93.

25. Ibid., p. 91.

26. Ibid., pp. 91-92.

27. William P. Young, *The Shack*, op. cit., p. 112.

28. Barbara Marx Hubbard, *The Revelation*, op. cit., p. 197.

29. Ibid., p. 267.

30. Ibid., p. 233.

31. Ibid., p. 255.

32. Ibid., p. 240.

33. *Messages From Maitreya the Christ*, op. cit., p. 248.

34. Ibid., p. 104.

Chapter 3: "God's Dream"—The Ultimate Scheme

1. Neale Donald Walsch, *Tomorrow's God: Our Greatest Spiritual Challenge*, op. cit., p. 262.

2. Neale Donald Walsch, "Should We Let Go of Our Dreams—A Message From God Channeled by Neale Donald Walsch" (Spirit Library, May 1, 2008, https://spiritlibrary.com/neale-donald-walsch/should-we-let-go-of-our-dreams).

3. Marianne Williamson, *Healing the Soul of America: Reclaiming Our Voices as Spiritual Citizens* (New York, NY: Touchstone, Simon & Schuster, 1997, 2000), p. 13; Editors of Martin Luther King, Jr. Papers Project, *The Papers of Martin Luther King, Jr.*, Volume III Birth

of a New Age (Berkeley, CA: University of California Press, 1997), p. 344.

4. Marianne Williamson, *Healing the Soul of America*, op. cit., p. 41; Editors of Martin Luther King, Jr. Papers Project, *The Papers of Martin Luther King, Jr.*, Volume III, op. cit., p. 458.

5. Marianne Williamson, *Healing the Soul of America*, op. cit., p. 33; Editors of Martin Luther King, Jr. Papers Project, The Papers of Martin Luther King, Jr., Volume III Birth of a New Age, op. cit., p. 342.

6. Marianne Williamson, *Healing the Soul of America*, op. cit., p. 41; Editors of Martin Luther King, Jr. Papers Project, The Papers of Martin Luther King, Jr., Volume III, op. cit., p. 456.

7. Rosemary Bray McNatt, "To Pray Without Apology: Why Martin Luther King Jr. Wasn't a Unitarian Universalist" (*UU World*, November/December 2002, http://archive.uuworld.org/2002/06/feature2.html).

8. Ibid.

9. Editors of Martin Luther King, Jr. Papers Project, *The Papers of Martin Luther King, Jr.*, Volume III, op. cit., pp. 340, 342, 456.

10. Ibid., p. 342.

11. Brian McLaren, *The Secret Message of Jesus: Uncovering the Truth That Could Change Everything* (Nashville, TN: W Publishing Group, 2006), p. 142.

12. This speech can be read at: http://www1.cbn.com/content/lou-engle-answering-call-dc.

13. David L. McKenna, Lloyd J. Ogilvie, General Editor, *The Preacher's Commentary:* Volume 17, Isaiah 1-39 (Nashville, TN: Thomas Nelson, 1993), p. 20.

14. Katherine Tingley, editor, "Practical Theosophy" (*New Century Path,* Volume VII, No. XIV, 1904, New Century Corporation, http://iapsop.com/archive/materials/century_path/new_century_path_v7_nov_1903-nov_1904.pdf), p. 922.

15. N. L., "Reincarnation" (*The Theosophical Path,* Volume X, No. 2, February 1916, New Century Corporation, Point Loma, CA., Katherine Tingley, editor, https://www.theosociety.org/pasadena/ttp/ttp_v10n02.pdf), p. 159.

16. *Britannica* online: https://www.britannica.com/topic/theosophy.

17. N. L., "Reincarnation" (*The Theosophical Path*, Volume X, No. 2, February 1916), op. cit., p. 159.

18. Paramahansa Yogananda, *Journey to Self-Realization: Collected Talks and Essays on Realizing God in Daily Life,* Volume 111 (Los Angeles, CA: Self-Realization Fellowship, 1997, 2005), p. 34.

19. Sri Chinmoy, *The Vision of God's Dawn,* taken from an extract called "God's Dream and God's Reality" (https://www.yogaofsrichinmoy.com/the-higher-worlds/dream/godsdreamreality).

20. *The Oprah Winfrey Show*, February 4, 1992.

21. *A Course in Miracles: Combined Volume*, op. cit. (Text), p. 125.

22. Ibid. (Text), p. 147.

23. Ibid. (Teachers Manual), p. 56.

24. Ibid. (Text), p. 344.

25. Ibid. (Text), p. 50.

26. Ibid. (Text), p. 14.

27. Ibid. (Text), pp. 377, 585.

28. Ibid. (Text), p. 584.

29. Dutch Sheets, "God Will Redeem His Dream" (https://m.youtube.com/watch?v=UKsEwBj8pXE), start at 3 minute 20 second mark.

30. Conrad Hanson, personal notes from author Johanna Michaelsen's telephone call to Crystal Cathedral on October 3, 1985, used with permission. More detail in Warren B. Smith's book *Deceived on Purpose: The New Age Implications of the Purpose Driven Church* (Mountain Stream Press, Second Edition, 2004), pp. 92-93.

31. "Reverend Sun Myung Moon Speaks on New Morning of Glory" (January 22, 1978 at Belvedere, New York, http://www.unification.net/1978/780122.html).

32. *Messages from Maitreya the Christ: One Hundred Forty Messages,* op. cit., p. 42.

33. Wayne Dyer, *You'll See It When You Believe It: The Way to Your Personal Transformation* (New York: NY: HarperCollins, First Quill Edition, 2001), pp. 108-109.

34. Neale Donald Walsch, "Should We Let Go of Our Dreams—A Message From God Channeled by Neale Donald Walsch" (Spirit

Library, May 1, 2008, https://spiritlibrary.com/neale-donald-walsch/should-we-let-go-of-our-dreams).

35. Ann Oldenburg, "The Divine Miss Winfrey" (*USA Today*, May 11, 2006, posted at www.religionnewsblog.com/14801/the-divine-miss-winfrey).

36. Oprah at the 2016 Essence Festival, New Orleans, Louisiana (https://www.youtube.com/watch?v=wUPKMiIeGhA).

37. Robert H. Schuller, *Your Church Has Real Possibilities* (Glendale, CA: Regal Book Division, G/L Publications, 1974), p. 177.

38. Robert H. Schuller, *Discover Your Possibilities* (New York, NY: Ballentine Books, 1978, 1990), p. 100.

39. Robert H. Schuller, *Self-Esteem: The New Reformation* (Waco, TX: Word Books, 1982), p. 75.

40. Ibid., p. 104.

41. Ibid., p. 112.

42. Richard Abanes, *Rick Warren and the Purpose That Drives Him: An Insider Looks at the Phenomenal Bestseller* (Eugene, OR: Harvest House Publishers, 2005), p. 94.

43. Rick Warren's Saddleback Church e-mail, October 27, 2003, "God's Dream for You—And the World!," op. cit.

44. Rick Warren, "How You Can Realize God's Dream for Your Life" (*Charisma* magazine, August 1, 2016, https://charismamag.com/spriritled-living/purposeidentity/how-you-can-realize-god-s-dream-for-your-life).

45. Rick Warren, "Dream Big" (*Daily Hope With Rick Warren*, July 30, 2016, https://www.crosswalk.com/devotionals/daily-hope-with-rick-warren/daily-hope-with-rick-warren-july-30-2016.html).

46. Ibid.

47. Rick Warren, "Dreaming the Future God Wants for You" (Saddleback Church sermon, February 16, 2020, https://saddleback.com/watch/time-to-dream/dreaming-the-future-god-wants-for-you), start at 38 minute 10 second mark.

48. Ibid., sermon notes on right-hand side of page.

49. Saddleback Church, October 26, 2003, Internet broadcast from Saddleback Church, transcribed by author, on file.

50. Bruce Wilkinson, *The Dream Giver* (Sisters, OR: Multnomah Publishers, Inc., 2003), p. 77.

51. Sarah Young, *Jesus Calling: Enjoying Peace in His Presence*, op. cit., p. 6.

52. Sarah Young (adapted by Tama Fortner), *Jesus Calling: 365 Devotions for Kids* (Nashville, TN: Tommy Nelson, 2010), p. 7.

53. Brian D. McLaren, *The Secret Message of Jesus: Uncovering the Truth That Could Change Everything* (Nashville, TN: W. Publishing Group, a Division of Thomas Nelson Inc., 2006), p. 142.

54. Ibid.

55. Shane Claiborne, *Jesus for President* (Grand Rapids, MI: Zondervan, 2008), p. 307.

56. Ravi Zacharias, keynote address at The Cannon House in Washington, D.C (National Day of Prayer Address on May 1, 2008, https://www.youtube.com/watch?v=Hcw9M1skHrI).

57. Ruth Malhotra, "Ravi Zacharias Participates in 67th Annual National Day of Prayer Observation in Washington, D.C." (This article is no longer available online, but his talk can be viewed at https://www.instagram.com/p/B_6ZQQF-0xoh/?hl=en.).

58. Catherine Meeks, editor, *Living Into God's Dream: Dismantling Racism in America* (New York, NY: Morehouse Publishing, 2016), p. vi.

59. Joel Osteen, "God's Dream for Your Life" (January 17, 2020, https://sermons-online.org/joel-osteen/joel-osteen-supersized).

60. Ann Schneible, "Synod Must Serve God's Dream, Not Try to 'Take Over,' Pope Says" (*Catholic News Agency*, October 5, 2014, https://www.catholicnewsagency.com/news/synod-must-serve-gods-dream-not-try-to-take-over-pope-says-37495).

61. Carol Glatz, "Pope Francis: God Wants People to Dream Big, Not Listen to Cynics" (*America Magazine: The Jesuit Review*, August 30, 2017, https://www.americamagazine.org/faith/2017/08/30/pope-francis-god-wants-people-dream-big-not-listen-cynics).

62. Pope Francis, "Lent with Pope Francis: "God's Dream for Us" (Franciscan Media, 3/18/18, https://www.franciscanmedia.org/franciscan-spirit-blog/lent-with-pope-francis-gods-dream-for-us).

63. Dr. Alan Keyes, "God's Dream for Us Is Better" (ChurchMilitant.com, June 9, 2020, https://www.churchmilitant.com/news/article/gods-dream-for-us-is-better).

64. Chip Ingram, "God's Dream for Your Life" (Living on the Edge, https://livingontheedge.org/broadcast/gods-dream-for-your-life).

65. Mark Batterson, *Chase the Lion: If Your Dream Doesn't Scare You, It's Too Small* (Sisters, OR: Multnomah, 2016, 2019), p. 4.

66. James Robison, "The Greatest Dream" (*The Stream,* April 4, 2018, https://stream.org/the-greatest-dream).

67. Sally Lloyd-Jones, *The Jesus Storybook Bible: Every Story Whispers His Name* (Grand Rapids, MI: Zonderkidz, 2007), p. 25.

68. Kenneth Copeland, "Dream Big Dreams" (Kenneth Copeland Ministries, Ministry Minute, https://blog.kcm.org/ministry-minute-dream-big-dreams).

69. Leonard Sweet, *soulTsunami*, op. cit., p. 34.

70. Richard Abanes, *Rick Warren and the Purpose That Drives Him*, op. cit., p. 94.

71. Bill Johnson, *Dreaming With God: Co-laboring With God for Cultural Transformation* (Shippensburg, PA: Destiny Image Publishers, Inc., 2006), p. 39.

72. Ibid., p. 21.

73. "God's Dream? A Kingdom Building Dream" (July 17, 2008, https://herescope.blogspot.com/2008/07/gods-dream.html?m=1).

74. Lou Engle Ministries (https://louengle.com).

75. Ibid.

76. Ibid.

77. Sean Feucht, *Fire and Fragrance* (Destiny Image Publishers, September 2010, Kindle edition), p. 198, Kindle location: 2387.

78. https://web.archive.org/web/20201027182143/https://www.fireandfragrance.ca/about.html.

79. https://www.burn24-7.com/about.

Chapter 4: Quantum Spirituality—Science Falsely So Called

1. Leonard Sweet's website: https://leonardsweet.com.

2. Warren B. Smith, *A "Wonderful" Deception: The Further New Age Implications of the Emerging Purpose Driven Movement* (Mountain Stream Press, 2009), p. 106.

3. Alice A, Bailey, *The Reappearance of the Christ*, op. cit., p. 150.

4. Benjamin Creme, *The Reappearance of the Christ and the Masters of Wisdom*, op. cit., p. 88.

5. Leonard Sweet, *soulTsunami*, op. cit., p. 28.

6. Leonard Sweet, *Quantum Spirituality*, op. cit., p. 125.

7. Leonard Sweet, *soulTsunami*, op. cit., p. 304.

8. Leonard Sweet, *Nudge: Awakening Each Other to the God Who Is Already There* (Colorado Springs, CO: David C. Cook, 2010), p. 157.

9. Ibid., p. 40.

10. Leonard Sweet, *Quantum Spirituality*, op. cit., p. 106.

11. Marilyn Ferguson, *The Aquarian Conspiracy: Personal and Social Transformation in the 1980s*, op. cit., p. 50.

12. Ibid., p. 25.

13. Pierre Teilhard de Chardin, *Christianity and Evolution*, op. cit., pp. 219-220.

14. Ibid,. p. 56.

15. Ibid,. p. 128.

16. Ibid,. p. 95.

17. Ibid,. p. 78.

18. Ibid,. p. 130.

19. Leonard Sweet, *Aqua Church: Essential Leadership Arts for Piloting Your Church in Today's Fluid Culture*, op. cit., p. 39.

20. Leonard Sweet and Frank Viola, *Jesus Speaks: Learning to Recognize & Respond to the Lord's Voice* (Nashville, TN: W Publishing Group, an imprint of Thomas Nelson, 2016), p. 85.

21. Leonard Sweet, *Quantum Spirituality*, op. cit., p. viii.

22. Willis Harman, *Global Mind Change: The New Age Revolution in the Way We Think* (New York, NY: Warner Books, 1988), front cover.

23. Matthew Fox, *The Coming of the Cosmic Christ: The Healing of Mother Earth and the Birth of a Global Renaissance* (San Francisco, CA: Harper & Row Publishers, 1988), p. 154.

24. Ibid., p. 137.

25. Leonard Sweet, *Quantum Spirituality*, op cit., pp. 124, 324.

26. M. Scott Peck, *The Road Less Traveled: A New Psychology of Love, Traditional Values and Spiritual Growth*, op. cit., p. 281.

27. Ibid.

28. M. Scott Peck, *The Different Drum: Community Making and Peace* (New York, NY: Simon & Schuster, 1988), pp. 205-206.

29. David Spangler and William Irwin Thompson, *Reimagination of the World: A Critique of the New Age, Science, and Popular Culture*, op. cit., p. 62.

30. Leonard Sweet, *Quantum Spirituality*, op. cit., p. 312.

31. Ibid., p. ix.

32. David Spangler, *The Revelation: Birth of A New Age* (Elgin, IL: Lorian Press, 1976), p. 177.

33. Leonard Sweet, *Quantum Spirituality*, op. cit., p. 312.

34. Leonard Sweet, *soulTsunami*, op. cit., p. 121.

35. David Spangler and William Irwin Thompson, *Reimagination of the World*, op. cit., p. 126.

36. *What the Bleep Do We Know!?* (DVD) (20th Century Fox, 2004, http://www.whatthebleep.com), transcribed by author.

37. Fritjof Capra, *The Tao of Physics: An Explanation of the Parallels Between Modern Physics and Eastern Mysticism* (Boston, MA: Shambhala Publications, Inc., 1999), p. 341.

38. Ibid.

39. *The Tides of Change: Riding the Next Wave in Ministry* (A 1995 audio presentation with Leonard Sweet and Rick Warren that was part of an ongoing series called "Choice Voices for Christian Leadership," distributed by Abington Press). On file (transcribed by author).

40. Leonard Sweet, *soulTsunami*, op. cit., p. 17.

41. Ibid., p. 34.

42. Leonard Sweet, *Quantum Spirituality*, op. cit., p. 125.

43. Leonard Sweet, *Nudge*, op. cit., p. 31.

44. Ibid., p. 40.

Chapter 5: Eugene Peterson's Mixed Message

1. "Eugene Peterson: A Monk Out of Habit," interview by Rodney Clapp (*Christianity Today*, April 3, 1987, Vol. 31, No. 6), p. 24.

2. Betty Lee Skinner, *Daws: A Man Who Trusted God* (Colorado Springs, CO: NavPress Publishing Group, 1974), pp. 153-155, 371.

3. *The Book of Proverbs KJV/The Message: Celebrating 400 Years of Scripture* (Colorado Springs, CO: NavPress, 2011), product description on Amazon.com.

4. Ronald S. Miller and the Editors of *New Age Journal, As Above, So Below: Paths to Spiritual Renewal in Daily Life,* op. cit., p. xi.

5. http://www.themystica.com/mystica/articles/a/below_above.html.

6. Neale Donald Walsch, *Friendship with God: an Uncommon Dialogue,* op. cit., pp. 295-296.

7. Michael J. Cusick, "A Conversation With Eugene Peterson" (*Mars Hill Review*, Fall 1995, Issue No. 3, www.marshillreview.com/sojo/peterson.shtm), pp. 73-90.

8. Benjamin Creme, *The Reappearance of the Christ and the Masters of Wisdom* (London, England: The Tara Press, 1980), p. 88.

9. Ibid., p. 30.

10. Ibid., p. 46.

11. https://en.wikipedia.org/wiki/Great_Work_(Hermeticism).

12. Maitreya, *Messages from Maitreya the Christ: One Hundred Forty Messages,* op. cit., p. 142.

13. Marianne Williamson, *Healing the Soul of America,* op. cit., p. 195.

14. Nick Sandberg, "The Great Work" (*Hidden Mysteries: The Magazine*, Vol. 14, July 2000, https://web.archive.org/web/20071029155053/www.hiddenmysteries.org/themagazine/vol14/articles/occult-notes.shtml).

15. Praise 96.5 FM (https://web.archive.org/web/20200924115210/https://www.praise965.com/music/brian-courtney-wilson-a-great-work-number-one-on-billboard-gospel-airplay-chart).

16. (https://m.youtube.com/watch?v=QYL-A1G9teE).

17. (https://www.thefreedictionary.com).

18. (http://www.freethesaurus.com).

19. (https://en.m.wikipedia.org/wiki/Lucifer_(magazine)#/media/File%3ABlavlucifer.jpg).

20. *The Light Bearer* (https://www.levir.com.br/theosophy/magazine.htm).

21. (https://bozemantc.org/tag/montana).

22. Amazon.com: "esoteric coffee mug-Lucifer the LIGHTBEARER."

23. (https://web.archive.org/web/20180126180351/https://www.aasrphasj.org/index.php/golden-circle).

24. (http://knights-of-the-golden-circle.blogspot.com).

25. (https://web.archive.org/web/20170309164831/http://www.angelfire.com/moon2/mystique_angel/AASB.html).

26. Ibid.

27. (https://sites.google.com/site/witcherymod/golden-chalk).

28. "New Age" (https://en.wikipedia.org/wiki/New_Age), citing Stephen J. Sutcliffe in *Children of the New Age* (London and New York: Routledge 2003), p. 128.

29. (https://web.archive.org/web/20080204113621/www.green-agenda.com/gaia.html).

30. Ann Moura, *Green Witchcraft* (Woodbury, MN: Lewellyn Publications, 2002).

31. (https://whisperingworlds.com/wiccan/wiccan_god.php).

32. "An Invitation to the Kingdom Coven" (Kingdom Coven YouTube, https://m.youtube.com/watch?v=F67U4dikvQE), 4:20 minute mark.

33. "The truth about the craft and Magick" (Kingdom Coven YouTube, https://m.youtube.com/watch?v=qos4H5g95CY), 3:00 minute mark.

34. William P. Young, *The Shack*, op. cit., p. 112.

35. Eugene Peterson, *Christ Plays in Ten Thousand Places* (Grand Rapids, MI: Eerdman's Publishing, 2005), p. 39.

36. Eugene Peterson, *The Jesus Way: A Conversation on the Ways That Jesus Is the Way* (Grand Rapids, MI: Wm. B. Erdman's Publishing Co., 2007), p. 131.

37. Ibid.

Chapter 6: Shack Theology—Universalism and Fractal Oneness

1. William P. Young, *The Shack*, op. cit., p. 112.

2. C. Baxter Kruger, *The Shack Revisited: There Is More Going on Here than You Ever Dared to Dream*, op. cit., p. xi.

3. Ibid., p. ix.

4. Sunny Shell, *"The Shack, a Biblical and Interactive Review"* (https://web.archive.org/web/20170319042606/http://blogs.christianpost.com/abandoned-to-christ/the-shack-a-biblical-and-interactive-review-28674, posted 2/16/17), quoting Paul Young from his August 15, 2007 blog

titled "*The Shack—update—Background #2*" (http://web.archive.org/web/20070911092057/; https://web.archive.org/web/20070911092057/http://www.windrumors.com/29/the-shack-update-background-2).

5. Sunny Shell, "*The Shack*, a Biblical and Interactive Review," op. cit., quoting Paul Young from his August 15, 2007 blog titled "Is the story of *The Shack* true . . . is Mack a "real" person? (http://web.archive.org/web/20070911092319/http://www.windrumors.com/30/is-the-story-of-the-shack-trueis-mack-a-real-person).

6. I have documented a short history of how this deceptive New Age teaching has entered the world and the church in chapter one of this book and in my booklet *Be Still and Know That You Are Not God*.

7. Wm. Paul Young, *Lies We Believe About God* (New York, NY: Atria Books, an imprint of Simon & Schuster, 2017), p. 118.

8. Ibid., p. 119.

9. Ibid., chapter 13 title in *Lies We Believe About God* is "You need to get saved."

10. Ibid., p. 118.

11. Ibid.

12. Ibid., p. 119.

13. William P. Young, *The Shack*, op. cit., p. 112.

14. In C. Baxter Kruger's book, *The Shack Revisited: There Is More Going On Here Than You Ever Dared to Dream*, in the foreword, *Shack* author William Paul Young writes: "I want to say, 'Thank you, and please read *The Shack Revisited.*'" He adds, "If you want to understand better the perspectives and theology that frame *The Shack*, this book is for you. Baxter has taken on the incredible task of exploring the nature and character of the God who met me in my own shack" (p. ix). On page 49 of *The Shack Revisited*, Kruger writes: "For inside of us all, because of Jesus, is nothing short of the very trinitarian life of God." C. Baxter Kruger, *The Shack Revisited: There Is More Going On Here Than You Ever Dared to Dream*, op. cit. p. 49.

15. William P. Young, *The Shack*, op. cit., p. 112.

16. C. Baxter Kruger, *The Shack Revisited*, op. cit., p. xi.

17. Khalil Gibran, *The Madman: His Parables and Poems* (Mineola, NY: Dover Publications, Inc., 2002, originally published in 1918 by Alfred A. Knopf, New York), p. 55.

18. John Dodge, "Kahlil Gibran and the Fall of the Prophet" (*Three Monkeys Online Magazine*, www.threemonkeysonline.com/kahlil-gibran-and-the-fall-of-the-prophet).

19. Liesl Schillinger, "Pioneer of the New Age" (*The New York Times*, December 13, 1998, http://www.nytimes.com/books/98/12/13/reviews/981213.13schillt.html).

20. Robin Waterfield, *Prophet: The Life and Times of Kahlil Gibran* (New York, NY: St. Martin's Press, 1998), p. 290.

21. Ibid., p. 289.

22. Wm. Paul Young, *Lies We Believe About God*, op. cit., p. 118.

23. Ibid., p. 119.

24. William P. Young, *The Shack*, op. cit., p. 112.

25. Oprah Winfrey, *Super Soul Sunday*, YouTube, July 9, 2017.

26. Wm. Paul Young personal blog, "I Want to Be More Like Oprah" (http://wmpaulyoung.com/i-want-to-be-more-like-oprah-watch-interview).

27. It should be noted that although Oprah Winfrey is an exceedingly powerful and influential New Age leader, she still persists in identifying herself as a Christian. But her Christianity is a New Age "Christianity" that is not biblically based and is therefore not Christianity at all.

28. William P. Young, *The Shack*, op. cit., p. 231.

29. Ibid., p. 11.

30. Ibid., p. 31.

31. C. Baxter Kruger, *The Shack Revisited*, op. cit., p. xi.

32. William P. Young, *The Shack*, op. cit., p. 136.

33. Michael Youssef, *The Shack Uncovered: 13 Heresies Explained* (Leading the Way Ministries, 2017, PDF: https://store.ltw.org/p-315-the-shack-uncovered-13-heresies-explained-pdf.aspx).

34. William P. Young, *The Shack*, op. cit., p.112.

35. Jennifer Pekich, "Fractal Theory in *The Shack*" (February 14, 2011, posted at: https://www.lighthousetrailsresearch.com/blog/?p=5701; used with author's permission), quoting in part from *The Shack*, op. cit., p. 129.

36. Referring to Larry DeBruyn. Visit his website at http://guardinghisflock.com.

37. "Fractal Chaos Crashes the Wall Between Science and Religion" (https://web.archive.org/web/20000307142346/http://www.fractal-wisdom.com/FractalWisdom/index.html).

38. Rick Warren, *The Purpose Driven Life*, op. cit., p. 248, quoted in: Warren Smith, *Deceived on Purpose*, op. cit., pp. 108-109.

39. "Fractal Chaos Crashes the Wall Between Science and Religion," op. cit., quoting Aldous Huxley.

40. Ibid.

41. Ibid.

42. William P. Young, *The Shack*, op. cit., p. 138.

43. Ibid., p. 112.

Chapter 7: The New Age Implications of *Jesus Calling*

1. Jim Fletcher, "Top Christian Bestseller Accused of Heresy" (WorldNetDaily, May 10, 2014, http://www.wnd.com/2014/05/top-christian-bestseller-accused-of-heresy).

2. Q&A with Sarah Young, Author Profile (The Christian Broadcasting Network http://www.cbn.com/entertainment/books/jesus-callingqa.aspx).

3. Two Listeners; Edited by A.J. Russell, *God Calling,* op. cit., p. 5.

4. John Ankerberg and John Weldon, *Encyclopedia of New Age Beliefs* (Eugene, OR: Harvest House Publishers, 1996), p. 103.

5. Ibid., p. 104.

6. Ibid., p. 80.

7. Sarah Young, *Jesus Calling: Enjoying Peace in His Presence*, op. cit., pp. Xl-XII, Printing 12 13 14 15 RRD 49 48 47 46.

8. Ruth Graham, "The Strange Saga of '*Jesus Calling,*' The Evangelical Bestseller You've Never Heard Of" (*The Daily Beast*, 02/23/14, http://www.thedailybeast.com/articles/2014/02/23/the-strange-saga-of-jesus-calling-the-evangelical-bestseller-you-ve-never-heard-of.html).

9. Sarah Young, *Jesus Calling,* op. cit., p. 94.

10. Ibid., p. Xll.

11. Victoria Neufeldt, Editor in Chief, *Webster's New World Dictionary: Third College Edition* (New York, NY: Simon & Schuster, Inc. 1988), p. 234.

12. Ibid., p. 389.

13. Sarah Young, *Jesus Calling;* 10*th* Anniversary Edition (Nashville, TN; Thomas Nelson Inc, 2004, 2011, 2014), Printing 14 15 16 17 18 DSC 5 4 3 2 1.

14. Sarah Young, *Jesus Calling*, op. cit., pp. X-Xl.

15. John Ankerberg and John Weldon, *Encyclopedia of New Age Beliefs*, op. cit., p. 578. Quoted from Dave Hunt and T.A. McMahon, *The Seduction of Christianity: Spiritual Discernment in the Last Days* (Eugene, OR: Harvest House Publishers, 1985), p. 123.

16. Sarah Young, *Jesus Calling,* 10*th* Anniversary Edition, op. cit.

17. Sarah Young, *Jesus Calling,* op. cit., p. 228.

18. Ibid., p. Xll.

19. Ibid., p. 362.

20. Ibid., p. 260.

21. Ibid., p. 139.

22. Ibid., p. 214.

23. Ibid., p. 241.

24. Ibid., p. 303.

25. Ibid., p. 85.

26. Ibid., p. 381.

27. Ibid., p. 209.

28. Ibid., p. 5.

29. Ibid., p. 360.

30. Ibid., p. 313.

31. Ibid., p. 260.

32. *Webster's New World Dictionary;* Third College Edition, op. cit., p. 937.

33. Edited by N.G.L. Hammond and H.H.Scullard, *The Oxford Classical Dictionary* (Oxford, UK: Oxford University Press, Second Edition, 1970), p. 36.

34. Ibid., pp. 36-37.

35. Marianne Williamson, *A Return to Love: Reflections on the Principles of A Course in Miracles* (New York, NY: Harper Perennial, 1996), p. 281.

36. Edited by N.G.L. Hammond and H.H. Scullard, *The Oxford Classical Dictionary,* op. cit., p. 37.

37. Barbara Marx Hubbard, *The Revelation: A Message of Hope for the New Millennium*, op. cit., p. 174.

38. Neale Donald Walsch, *The New Revelations: A Conversation with God*, op. cit., p. 157.

39. Victoria Neufeldt, Editor in Chief, *Webster's New World Dictionary*; Third College Edition, op. cit., p. 273.

40. Sarah Young, *Jesus Calling*, op. cit., p. 362.

41. Barbara Marx Hubbard, *The Revelation*, op. cit., p. 264.

42. Sarah Young, *Jesus Calling*, op. cit., p. 6.

43. Sarah Young (adapted by Tama Fortner), *Jesus Calling: 365 Devotions For Kids*, op. cit., p. 7.

44. *New Century Path*, Volume VII, No. XIV, 1904, p. 16. Katherine Tingley, Editor, New Century Corporation, Point Loma, CA. (https://books.google.com/books?id=IDxDAQA-AIAAJ&pg=RA2-PA).

45. Ann Oldenburg, "The Divine Miss Winfrey" (*USA Today*, May 10, 2006, http://www.usatoday.com/life/people/2006-05-10-oprah_x.htm).

46. Wayne Dyer, *You'll See it When You Believe It: The Way to Your Personal Transformation* (New York, NY: HarperCollins, First Quill Ed., 2001), p. 108.

47. Sri Chinmoy; late resident Indian guru at the United Nations (http://www.yogaofsrichinmoy.com/god_the_author_all_good/mangod).

48. Desmond Tutu, "Archbishop Desmond Tutu Speech" (March 18, 2004, Bender Arena at American University, http://wwwl.media,american.edu/speeches/desmondtutu.htm).

49. Robert H. Schuller, *Your Church Has Real Possibilities* (Glendale, CA: Regal Books Division, G/L Publications, 1974), pp. 176-179.

50. Rick Warren, Saddleback Church e-mail, October 27, 2003, "GOD'S DREAM FOR YOU—AND THE WORLD!"; Warren Smith, *Deceived on Purpose: The New Age Implications of the Purpose-Driven Church* (Mountain Stream Press, 2004), pp. 131-142.

51. Brian McLaren, *The Secret Message of Jesus: Uncovering the Truth that Could Change Everything*, op. cit., p. 161.

52. Joel Osteen, "God's Dream for Your Life"—Joel Osteen Ministries daily devotional 28 July Monday" (http://devotion.

wedaretobelieve.com/2014/07/gods-dream-for-your-life-joel-osteen.html).

53. Bruce Wilkinson, *The Dream Giver*, op. cit., p. 77.

54. Leonard Sweet, *soulTsunami: Sink or Swim in the New Millennium Culture*, op. cit., p. 34.

55. Ann Oldenburg, "The Divine Miss Winfrey" (*USA Today*, May 10, 2006, http://www.usatoday.com/life/people/2006-05-10-oprah_x.htm).

56. Joel Osteen, *Wake Up to Hope* (New York, NY: FaithWords. Hachette Book Group, 2016, Kindle Edition), p. 316, Kindle location: 3346. Also at: https://www.facebook.com/JoelOsteen/posts/10156779974255227.

57. Sarah Young (adapted by Tama Fortner), *Jesus Calling: 365 Devotions For Kids*, op. cit. p. 7.

58. Rick Warren, Saddleback Church e-mail, October 27, 2003, "GOD'S DREAM FOR YOU—AND THE WORLD!," op. cit.

59. Brian McLaren, *The Secret Message of Jesus*, op cit., p. 161.

60. Leonard Sweet, *soulTsunami*, op. cit., p. 34.

61. Sarah Young, *Dear Jesus: Seeking His Light in Your Life* (Nashville, TN: Thomas Nelson, Inc., 2007), pp. 68-69; Sarah Young: *Jesus Lives: Seeing His Love in Your Life* (Nashville, TN: Thomas Nelson, 2009), p. 124; Sarah Young (adapted by Tama Fortner), *Jesus Calling: 365 Devotions For Kids*, op. cit., p. 7.

62. Sarah Young, *Jesus Calling*, op. cit., p. 199.

63. Sarah Young, *Jesus Calling* (original introduction), op. cit., pp. VII-VIII.

64. Sarah Young, *Jesus Calling* (revised introduction, 10th Anniversary Edition), op. cit., p. xiv.

Chapter 8: A False New Age Christ—What We Can Learn

1. April 25, 1982: *New York Times* and many other major newspapers around the world.

2. Wayne S. Peterson, *Extraordinary Times, Extraordinary Beings: Experiences of an American Diplomat with Maitreya and the Masters of Wisdom* (Henderson, NV: Emergence Press, 2001), p. 35.

3. Benjamin Creme, *Maitreya's Mission*, Volume Two, op. cit., p. 15.

4. Wayne S. Peterson, *Extraordinary Times, Extraordinary Beings,* op. cit., p. 100.

5. Wayne S. Peterson interviewed on *Bridging Heaven & Earth,* a weekly talk show broadcast on Cox Communications' public access channel 17 in Santa Barbara, California on November 9, 2001, Videocassette (http://www.HeaventoEarth.com).

6. (https://abcnews.go.com/Business/economist-raj-patel-messiah/story?id=10228530).

7. Wikipedia: Buccus, Imraan (23 March 2011). "World Class Intellectual Engagement" *The Mercury.*

8. *Messages from Maitreya the Christ: One Hundred Forty Messages,* op. cit., p. 6.

9. Ibid., p. 248.

10. Ibid., p. 62.

11. Benjamin Creme, *The Reappearance of the Christ and the Masters of Wisdom,* op. cit., p. 30.

12. Ibid., p. 85.

13. Ibid., p. 46.

14. Warren B. Smith, *Eugene Peterson's Mixed Message: Subversive Bible for a New Age* (Roseburg, OR: Lighthouse Trails Publishing, 2019, online at: https://www.lighthousetrailsresearch.com/blog/?p=29709).

15. *Messages from Maitreya the Christ,* op. cit., p. 159.

16. Ibid., p. 266.

17. Ibid., p. 123.

18. Ibid., p. 206.

19. Ibid., p. 183.

20. Ibid., p. 192.

21. Ibid., p. 153.

22. Ibid., p. 56.

23. Benjamin Creme, *Maitreya's Mission,* Volume Two, op. cit., p. 717.

24. Keyworth Ngosa, *Ultimate Deception: The Purpose Driven Life Is the Satanic Great Invocation* (Johannesburg, South Africa: Full Armour Ministries, 2019).

25. Benjamin Creme, *The Reappearance of the Christ and the Masters of Wisdom,* op. cit., p. 135.

26. Alice A. Bailey, *The Reappearance of the Christ* (New York, NY: Lucis Publishing Company,1948), p. 150.

27. Tom Holladay and Kay Warren, *Foundations Participant's Guide: 11 Core Truths To Build Your Life On* (Grand Rapids, MI: Zondervan, 2003), p. 46.

28. Ibid.

29. Benjamin Creme, *The Reappearance of the Christ and the Masters of Wisdom,* op. cit., p. 37.

30. (https://www.share-international.org/archives/M_appearances/faq_M_appearances.htm).

31. Benjamin Creme, *Maitreya's Mission,* Volume Two, op. cit., p. 250.

32. Warren Smith, "Holy Laughter or Strong Delusion?" (SCP Newsletter, Volume 19:2, Fall 1994); Warren Smith, *False Revival Coming: Holy Laughter or Strong Delusion?* (Roseburg, OR: Lighthouse Trails Publishing, 2015, online at: https://www.lighthousetrailsresearch.com/blog/?p=16760).

33. Barbara Marx Hubbard, *Teachings From the Inner Christ: for Founders of a New Order of the Future (A Work in Progress): A Complement to the Book of Co-Creation* (Greenbrae, CA: Foundation For Conscious Evolution, 1994), p. 79.

34. Barbara Marx Hubbard, *The Revelation: A Message of Hope for the New Millennium,* op. cit., p. 243.

35. *A Course in Miracles: Combined Volume,* op. cit. (Teacher's Manual), p. 37.

Chapter 9: Global Revival or Global Deception? 10 Critical Warnings

1. William J. Broad, "Toppling Theories, Scientists Find 6 Slits, Not Big Gash, Sank *Titanic*" (*New York Times*, April 8, 1997, https://www.nytimes.com/1997/04/08/science/toppling-theories-scientists-find-6-slits-not-big-gash-sank-titanic.html).

2. Walter Lord, *The Night Lives On* (New York, NY: Avon Books, 1986, 1987), p. 1.

3. Rick Warren, Saddleback Church e-mail, October 27, 2003, "God's Dream for You—And the World!"—On file.

4. N. L., "Reincarnation" (*The Theosophical Path*, Volume X, No. 2, February 1916), p. 159. Also read Warren B. Smith's booklet, *God's Dream* online at: https://www.lighthousetrailsresearch.com/blog/?p=28521.

5. Robert Hough, "God Is Alive and Well and Saving Souls on Dixon Road" (*Toronto Life* magazine, February 1995), p. 31; cited in James A. Beverley, *Holy Laughter and The Toronto Blessing* (Grand Rapids, MI: Zondervan Publishing House, 1995), p. 12.

6. Michael Brown, *From Holy Laughter to Holy Fire: America on the Edge of Revival* (Shippensburg, PA: Destiny Image Publishers, 1996), p. 18.

7. John Arnott, "The Toronto Blessing: What Is It?" (John & Carol, December 31, 1999, www.johnandcarol.org/updates/the-toronto-blessing-what-is-it).

8. Leonard Sweet, *soulTsunami: Sink or Swim in New Millennium Culture*, op. cit., p. 34.

9. Barbara Marx Hubbard, *The Revelation: A Message of Hope for the New Millennium*, op. cit., pp. 157, 172-173.

10. Chris Mitchell, "Spirit-Empowered Believers Praying for a Second Pentecostal Outpouring" (*Charisma* magazine, https://www.charismamag.com/spirit/revival/20088-spirit-empowered-believers-praying-for-second-pentecostal-outpouring).

11. Barbara Marx Hubbard, *The Revelation,* op. cit., p. 243.

12. Benjamin Creme, *Maitreya's Mission*, Volume Two, op. cit., p. 250.

13. *A Course in Miracles: Combined Volume*, op. cit. (Teacher's Manual), p. 37.

14. Walter Lord, *A Night to Remember* (New York, NY: St. Martin's Griffin, 1955, 1983), p. 12.

15. Leonard Sweet, *Quantum Spirituality: A Postmodern Apologetic,* op. cit., p. viii.

16. Fritjof Capra, *The Tao of Physics: An Exploration of the Parallels Between Modern Physics and Eastern Mysticism*, op. cit., p. 341.

17. Leonard Sweet, *Quantum Spirituality,* op. cit., p. 125.

18. United States Senate Inquiry (*Titanic* Inquiry Project, https://www.titanicinquiry.org/USInq/USReport/AmInqRep04.php).

19. "Wreck of the White Star Liner *Titanic*: How the World's Greatest Steamship Went Down With 1,600 Souls" (*Scientific American*, April 27, 1912, Vol. CVI, No. 17, https://www.scientificamerican. com/article/archive-titanic-wreck-white-star-liner).

20. Nick Barratt, *Lost Voices From the Titanic: The Definitive Oral History* (New York, NY: Palgrave Macmillan, 2010), pp. 131-132.

21. Bill Johnson, *Dreaming With God, Co-laboring With God for Cultural Transformation* (Shippensburg, PA: Destiny Image Publishers, Inc., 2006), p. 179.

22. Walter Lord, *A Night to Remember*, op. cit., p. 11.

23. Ibid., p. 13.

24. Geoff Tibballs, editor, *Voices From the Titanic, The Epic Story of the Tragedy From the People Who Were There* (New York, NY: Skyhorse Publishing, 2012), p. 67.

25. Lawrence Beesley, *The Loss of the S.S. Titanic, Its Story and Its Lessons* (New York, NY: A Mariner Book, Houghton Mifflin Company, 1912, 2000), p. 109.

26. Julia Duin, "Praise the Lord and Pass the New Wine" (*Charisma* magazine, August 1994).

27. Randy Clark, *Lighting Fires* (Mechanicsburg, PA: Global Awakening, 2011, Kindle edition; originally published in 1998 by Charisma Media), Kindle location: 1645-1646.

28. Ibid.

29. Brian McLaren, *The Secret Message of Jesus: Uncovering the Truth That Could Change Everything*, op. cit., p. 144.

30. Rick Warren's e-mail on file with Spiritual Research Network.

31. Sarah Young, *Jesus Calling: Enjoying Peace in His Presence*, op. cit., p. 16.

32. See *The New Age Implications of "Jesus Calling"* online at: https:// www.lighthousetrailsresearch.com/blog/?p=16568.

33. See *Changing "Jesus Calling": Damage Control for a False Christ* online at: https://www.lighthousetrailsresearch.com/blog/?p=16349.

34. William Stead, *After Death: Letters From Julia* (Woodland, CA: Ancient Wisdom Communications, public domain, originally published 1905), p. 21.

35. Estelle Wilson Stead, *My Father, Personal & Spiritual Reminiscences* (London, England: William Heinemann, 1913, reprinted by Hard Press Publishing), p. 300.

36. William Stead, *After Death: Letters From Julia*, op. cit., p. 29.

37. Estelle Wilson Stead, *My Father, Personal & Spiritual Reminiscences*, op. cit., p. 279. *The Welsh Revival & The Story of the Welsh Revival by Eyewitnesses,* (Lawton: OK, Trumpet Press, 2015). Originally this book was two independent books both published in 1905: William T. Stead authoring *The Welsh Revival* and "eyewitnesses" authoring *The Story of the Welsh Revival.*

38. "Endorsements and Contacting the Endorsers" (Spiritual Research Network, https://www.spiritualresearchnetwork.org/have-heart-bridging-the-gulf-between-heaven-and-earth-endorsements.html), per Chris Lawson, president of the Spiritual Research Network, telephone call with Steve Berger regarding *Have Heart.*

39. Ibid., per Chris Lawson, pertaining to his telephone call with Greg Laurie's secretary about *Have Heart.*

40. Steve Berger's Facebook page, September 26, 2020.

41. Promise Keepers (https://promisekeepers.org/promise-keepers/about-us/board-members and https://promisekeepers.org/promise-keepers/about-us/pastoral-advisory-board).

42. (https://beholdisrael.org/event/awaiting-his-return-nashville).

43. William Stead, *After Death: Letters From Julia*, op. cit., p. 29.

44. James Redfield, *The Twelfth Insight: The Hour of Decision* (New York, NY: Grand Central publishing, 2011), p. 179.

45. Steven Biel, editor, *Titanica: The Disaster of the Century in Poetry, Song, and Prose* (New York, NY: W.W. Norton & Company, 1998), pp. 25-26.

46. *Your Dictionary* (https://www.yourdictionary.com/convergence).

47. Pierre Teilhard de Chardin, *Christianity and Evolution*, op. cit., p. 130.

48. Ibid.

49. Leonard Sweet, *Quantum Spirituality*, op. cit., p. 106.

50. Leonard Sweet, *soulTsunami*, op., cit., p. 23.

51. Leonard Sweet, *AquaChurch: Essential Leadership Arts for Piloting Your Church in Today's Fluid Culture*, op. cit., taken from subtitle.

Epilogue

1. Samuel J. Andrews, *Christianity and Anti-Christianity in Their Final Conflict* (Bend, OR: The Berean Call edition, 2017; originally published in New York and London by G. P. Putnam's Sons in 1898, 1899), p. vii-xxi.

2. Ibid., p. 17.

Index

OTHER BOOKS BY WARREN B. SMITH

The Light That Was Dark: From the New Age to Amazing Grace

False Christ Coming—Does Anybody Care?: What New Age Leaders Really Have in Store for America, the Church, and the World

Deceived on Purpose: The New Age Implications of the Purpose-Driven Church

A "Wonderful" Deception: The Further New Age Implications of the Emerging Purpose Driven Movement

"Another Jesus" Calling: How Sarah Young's False Christ is Deceiving the Church

Pressing On Through It All: Scriptural Encouragement for These Last Days

Watering the Greyhound Garden: Stories From the Streets of San Francisco

The Titanic and Today's Church: A Tale of Two Shipwrecks

E-mail: warren@mountainstreampress.org
Website: www.newagetoamazinggrace.com
YouTube: https://www.youtube.com/warrenbsmith

Warren B. Smith's books can be ordered through most bookstores and major outlets (including Amazon) as well as www.newagetoamazinggrace.com. Digital formats also available. For toll free ordering, call 866-876-3910.

Made in the USA
Monee, IL
07 July 2026

56549102R00125